I0016123

Fedora

Precise

Version 29

Shiv Kumar Goyal

Preface

This book is for system administrators or Linux enthusiast. This book is written keeping in mind practical aspects of Fedora Linux. I will call this book as no non sense book. If you are plaining to deploy Fedora Linux or you are maintaining Fedora machine than this book is for you. All procedures written in the book are to the point with available screen shots and output samples This book leaves no stone unturned to cover all practical parts of Linux administration. If you are short of time and hates reading bulky books, then this book is for you it covers all articles from basics to advance level.

This book examines Fedora Linux for server administrators. Main emphasis is on what a user would need to know to perform particular task. The focus here is on day to day challenges faced by administrators and users. The book covers topics like desktops, shell commands, and network tools. Administration topics are also covered including user management, software management, repositories, services, system monitoring, shell configuration, network connections, SELinux, firewalls and configuration of different servers like HTTP, FTP, NTP etc. This is book is excellent choice for preparing interview. I tried my level best to keep the text as precise as possible. If you are Red Hat, Centos, Oracle Linux or scientific Linux user than this book will also help you as lot of the procedure are same as Fedora Linux.

I hope you will like this book

Thanks

Shiv Kumar Goyal

Table of Contents

## Chapter 1

Introduction

Linux is UNIX like Operating system. Linux is an open source project started by Linus Torvalds in 1991. There are thousands of Linux distributions in the market, but broadly can be classified on their root distribution for example Centos, Oracle and Scientific Linux based on Redhat which in turn based on Fedora Linux. Fedora Linux is community project sponsored by Red Hat.

Free V/s Paid

Linux although is open source project but there are two types of Linux distribution available one is free and other is paid. Free is self-explanatory you do not have to pay anything. If you have any problem, you can take help of volunteers working for Linux community. However, problem is that this type of support is not time bond as it is given voluntarily. For corporate sector where you have limited number of Linux resources, it is a big problem. So companies who uses mission critical Linux servers and computers prefers paid type of Linux Distribution where they pay fixed amount as subscription and support fee. These paid Linux distribution companies keeps team of Linux experts to provide support and fixes.

The prominent player in free Linux are Ubuntu, Debian, Fedora, Opensuse etc. Red hat and SUSE is major player in non- free enterprise Linux distribution.

Package types

There are two ways to distribute packages for application installation on the Linux.

Using source code

This is hard way to install software in which you use source code provided by developer to install the software. As this is source code written in native language you have to first compile and then use it.

Using packages

All modern Linux distribution uses packages stored in repositories. There is difference between different Linux Distribution how they distribute their installation packages, Red hat and SUSE uses RPM package based distribution where as Debian based distribution like Ubuntu, Mint Linux are of DEB packaging.

Fedora and Red hat

Fedora is free distribution and community project sponsored by Red hat. Fedora is upstream for Red hat enterprise Linux. Fedora is test bed for new features, which may get incorporate in upcoming Red hat Linux version. Main difference between the Fedora Linux and Red hat Enterprise Linux is support and life cycle of the product. Red hat is commercially supported product whereas Fedora is community supported. Red hat Enterprise Linux has life cycle of few years and supported up to 10 years but in case of Fedora new release come out after every 6 months and gets update for 13 months only. Fedora is free product with bleeding edge technologies incorporated in it. So if you want to experience new upcoming features then Fedora is for you.

## Chapter 2

Minimum system requirement

Following are minimum requirement to install Fedora Linux. However, it is ideal to have more resources than this for optimum working of applications

Processor   1GHz or faster

System memory (RAM)   1GB

Hard disk   10GB

Graphical installation of Fedora requires a minimum screen resolution of 800x600. If you have device with lower resolution you should use VNC installation.

GNOME3 is the default desktop environment for fedora 29 workstation. it preforms better with hardware acceleration. However, you can also install other desktop environment like KDE, Mate, LXDE, LXQt, Cinnamon.

## Chapter 3

New Features in Fedora Version 29

Fedora 29 has introduced so many new features. The main improvements are :-

1. **GNOME 3.30**

With Fedora 29 you will get GNOME 3.30 Release

2. **DNF 4**

   New version of DNF version 4 has been introduced in version 29 with following additional features

   - A new module dependency resolver.
   - A new history database.
   - Pseudo-modules support.

3. **Python 3.7**
4. **Samba 4.9**
5. **Management of thunderbolt devices**
6. **Management of encrypted disks using Disks utility**
7. **Liberation fonts 2.0**
8. **Rubby on Rails 5.2**
9. **Kubernetes Modules**
10. **GNU C library version 3.28**
11. **OpenShift Origin 3.11**

## Chapter 4

Installation

In this chapter we will covers installation of Fedora Linux version 29. The installation of fedora is very easy and straight forward. This chapter is designed in such way even if you do not have prior knowledge of Linux you can install Fedora easily as whole installation is explained step by step with screenshots.

Installation of Fedora includes following steps

1. **Select the media type**

   There are three types of media is available. Select media according to role your machine will play.

   1. Server
   2. Workstation
   3. Atomic (For Cloud computing)

2. **Download Media Image**

   Once you decided machine role, it's time to download the installation image. You can download the image directly if internet connection is stable otherwise you can download using torrent client. You can download image from **https://getfedora.org** fedora site.

3. **Verify image**

   Once you finish downloading of installation image, it is good practice to verify the integrity of the downloaded image.

4. Write image to media.

5. Select way how you want install it. There are two common ways to install: -

   1. **Interactive**

      Interactive method is normal installation method which can be either Text based or GUI. This method of installation requires user interaction for inputs.

   2. **Automated using Kickstart**

      For Kickstart installation, we have to create a single file containing the answers to all the questions fedora installation normally asks during interactive installation. Once the installation starts, no user intervention is required.

6. Verify the installation.

Interactive installation

Bellow mentioned steps are for fedora server installation. But if you want to install fedora workstation the steps are almost same. If you use fedora server DVD then you will not get GUI interface. Workstation media provides Graphical desktop after installation

Downloading

To start installation first download media from https://getfedora.org

If stable internet is not available, you can download torrent file from https://torrent.fedoraproject.org/

Fedora-Server-dvd-x86_64-29.torrent	Fedora Server dvd x86_64 29

After torrent file is downloaded. Use this file to add torrent in torrent client like utorrent, bit torrent, transmission etc.

Verifying downloaded image

Once file has been downloaded check the integrity of file. If you downloaded file on MS Windows computer, you can download free **File Checksum Integrity Verifier tool** from site

https://raylin.wordpress.com/downloads/md5-sha-1-checksum-utility/

7

Run this utility and select file and select sha256 and verify now match number with sha256 checksum from site https://getfedora.org/verify .

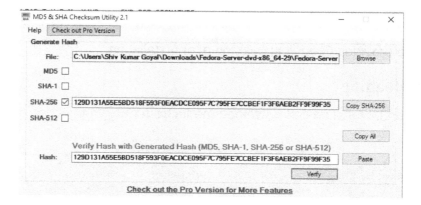

Write image to media

After verification of image you can write the ISO file to DVD. If DVD Drive in your computer is not working or not present you can write this image to USB flash drive.

Creating USB Media on Windows

1. Download media writer from
   https://github.com/MartinBriza/MediaWriter/releases.

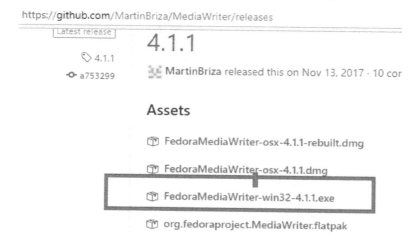

2. Double click the downloaded file to install it and follow the Wizard.

3. Once installation is finished run the file. From the menu select **Custom image**.

4. Select image and plug the USB flash media. Once it is ready press **Write**.

5. Now flash is ready

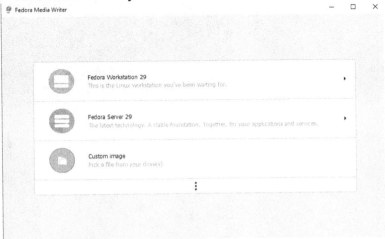

Booting with Media

Once media is ready. Make media as first boot device in BIOS of computer. Check the manual of your computer to change boot priority. Once system boots, Installation menu will come, Select **Install Fedora Linux 29**

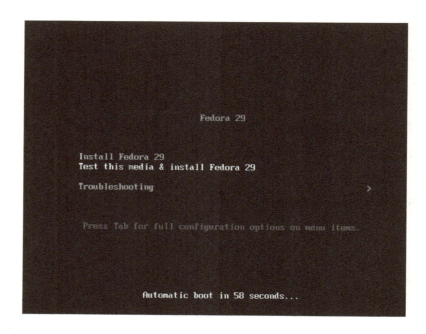

1. Select Language and press **continue**

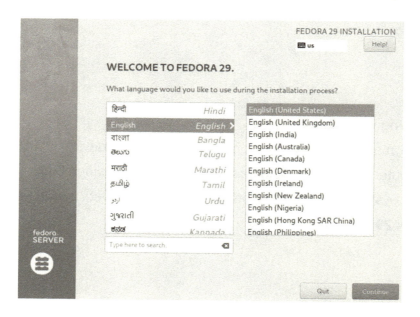

2. This brings **Installation Summary** Screen. Here you can customize your installation. This screen gives you option to change keyboard, language, Time, date, installation source, storage, software and network configuration.

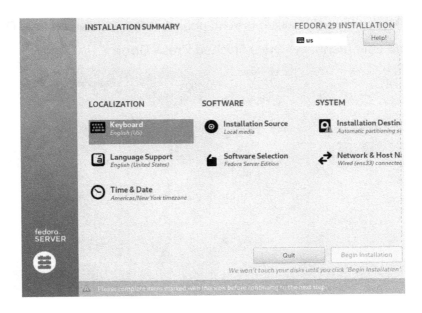

3. Select **keyboard,** change it, if required and press **Done** When Finished.

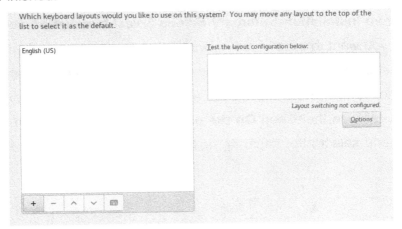

4. From **Installation Summary** screen, select **Time and Date**. Select **Time zone** where machine is located. You can change **Network Time** switch to **ON** position for using internet or local time server to provide date and time sync. If network server is in **ON** position then you can press gear sign for providing custom network server. If Network server switch is in off position then you can change Date and time manually. Once finished Press **Done**

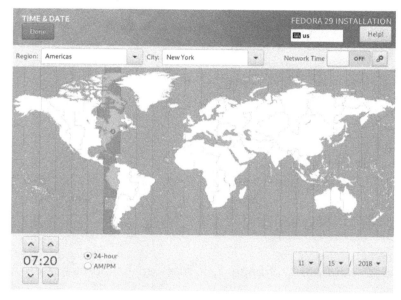

5. From **Installation Summary** Screen Select **Installation source**. If you want to install from network you can select here. If you are installing from internet you can select **On the network** and keep Closest Mirror selected. If you are using your own local server for installation then keep **On the network** selected, from drop down menu select http, https, ftp or NFS server and enter server's IP

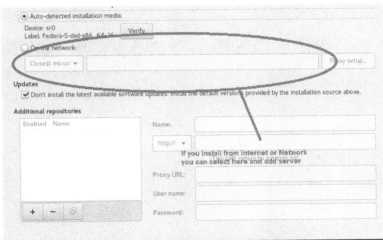

address or domain name in text box. When finished press **Done**. In our case it is from DVD so no need to change.

6. Click **Software selection** from Installation Summary screen and select the required software. I am keeping it as default, We can add additional required software after installation also. Press **Done** after selection.

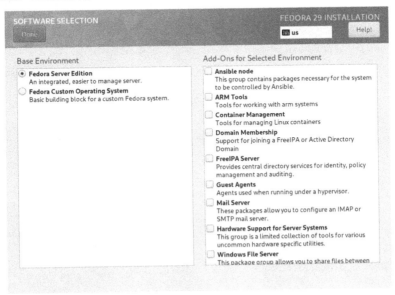

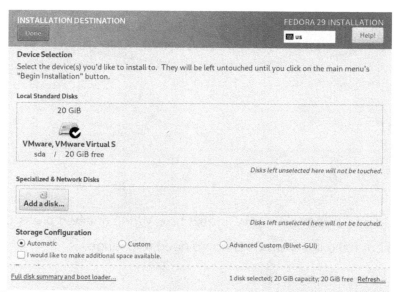

7. From **Installation Summary**, select **Installation destination**. Either leave it to **Automatic** in storage configuration for partitioning

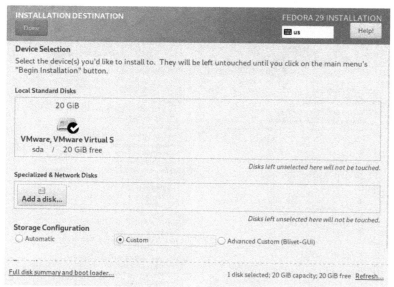

the disk automatically.

For specific requirement of partitioning, select **Custom.** For demonstration purpose in this installation, I am selecting Custom storage configuration.

On the manual partitioning screen select **Standard partition**.

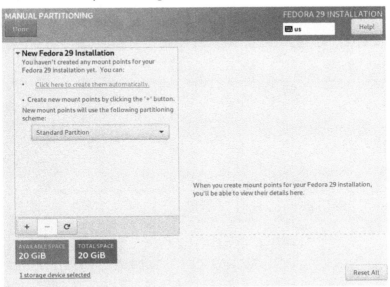

After selecting partitioning scheme, press "**+**" Button to add partition. Select "**/**" from drop down menu for root partition and give Desired capacity in this example we give 10GB.

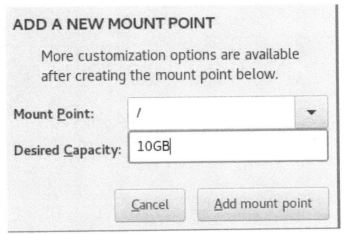

Desired capacity can be written in human readable language like MB GB if you want 900 MB you will write 900MB or in this example 10 GB as 10GB after finishing press **Add Mount point.**

Same way add Swap, home and boot partition. Swap partition should be of equal to or more than physical RAM of the system. Boot partition can be of 500MB Note:

ADD A NEW MOUNT POINT

More customization options are available after creating the mount point below.

Mount Point: /boot

Desired Capacity: 500MB

Cancel   Add mount point

If you have selected BTRFS as file system you have to create boot partition separate as till now fedora doesn't support BTRFS as boot partition when you create separate boot partition it will change its partition type to EXT.

After adding partition Press Done.

It will Show **Summary of Changes** screen press Accept changes

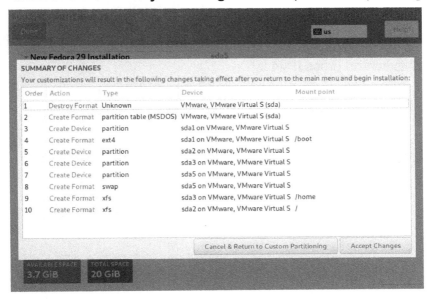

8. From **Installation Summary** screen Click on **Configure network and hostname**. First change **Hostname** and press **Apply**. Host Name is name of computer which it is recognized on the network.

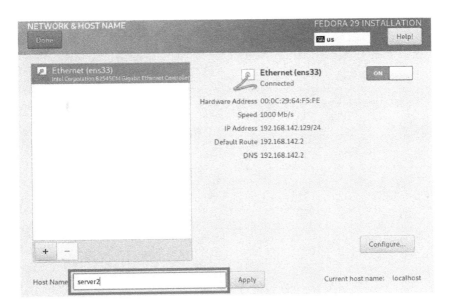

9. If you have static IP address, then click configure button. For demonstration purpose I will configure with static address.

10. On pressing **Configure**, **Edit Network card** screen will come. On this screen press **IPv4** tab.

11. On IPv4 Tab select method as **Manual** from drop down menu.

12. Select **Add** and provide IP address, Netmask, Gateway and DNS server. Press **Save** after finishing.

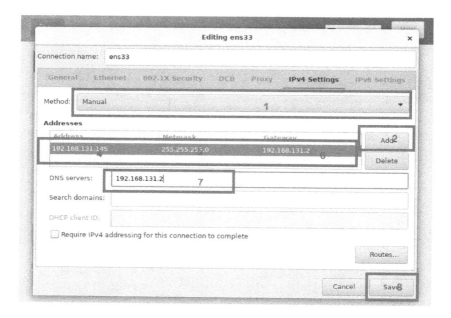

13. Select **General** Tab and make sure **Automatically connect to this network when it is available** is clicked then Press **Save**. You will come back to network configuration screen press **Done**

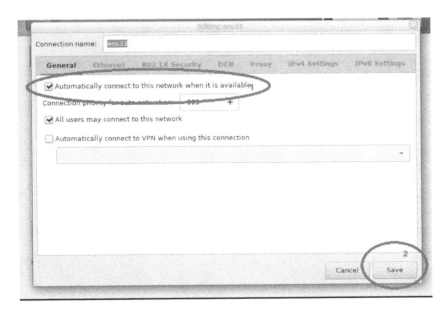

14. Now customization part is finished. Just review all changes on **Installation summary** screen press **Begin installation**.

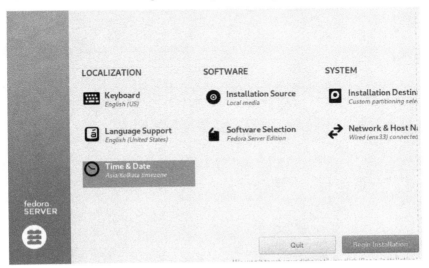

15. This will bring to Configuration screen. Here you can set root (Administrator) password and create one more user.

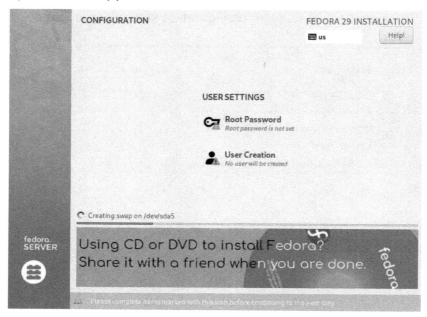

16. Select root password and set root password. Press **Done.**

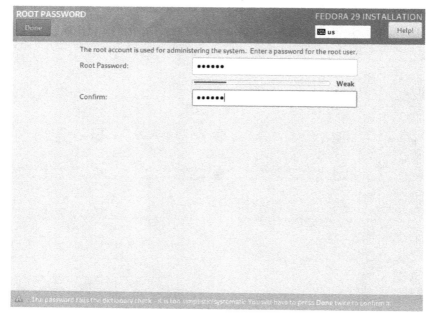

17. Select user creation. Give User's Full name, User name and password.

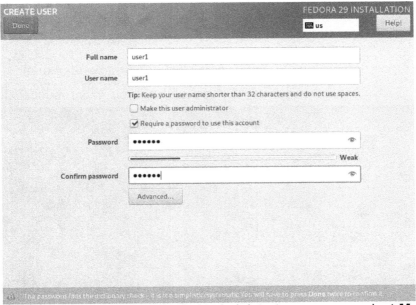

If you want to use this user as administrator, you can select **Make this user administrator**. After that press **Done**.

18. System will start copping files. Once copping is finished press **Reboot.**

19. After reboot you will see bellow screen. Congratulation your installation is finished now.

20. Once server finishes booting you will get command line interface to work on the server. Congratulation you have successfully

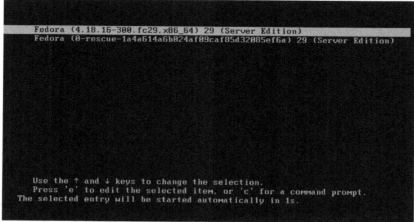

installed fedora 29 server.

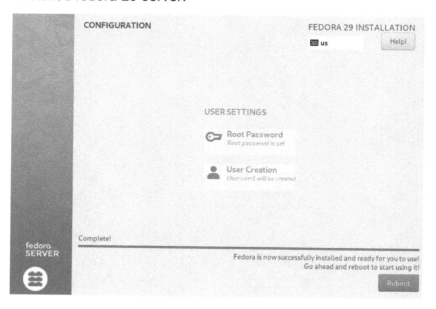

## Chapter 5

Connecting Your PC to Fedora Server

In practical life you occasionally work on server, usually you connect from your PC and do administration. You may be using MS windows 7 or MS windows 10. First thing you require to connect to Linux host is a software. There are many options like VanDyke, bitvise and putty. Among them putty is free and very popular option. To install putty open internet explorer and download putty from

http://www.chiark.greenend.org.uk/~sgtatham/putty/latest.html

Once you have downloaded the putty install it.

When you start putty you will see following screen. On this screen

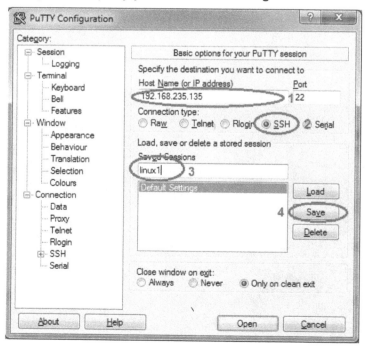

1. Write the IP Address of the newly installed server.

2. Select the Protocol as **SSH**
3. Give name of Session like fedora1 or linux1 etc.
4. Press **Save** button

Once session is saved either double click the session name to connect to the Linux host or select the session press **Load** then press **Open**

## Chapter 6

Configuring Graphical User Interface

If you have installed Fedora Workstation then you will get GUI by default, but if you have installed the Fedora server then you will not get GUI environment by default. Some administrator like to work in Graphical user Interface environment or some projects require graphical desktop. In that case you have to add graphical interface to your fedora server. To add graphical desktop environment to your server do following steps: -

1. Login as **root** user
2. Give command **dnf group install 'fedora workstation'**

```
# dnf groupinstall 'fedora workstation'
```
   it will confirm you to install additional software

3. Once installation complete, give command **systemctl set-default graphical.target** to change default target

```
# systemctl set-default graphical.target
```

4. Now enable gdm service to start automatically using command **systemctl enable gdm.service**

```
# systemctl enable gdm.service
```

5. Reboot the server it will restart in GUI mode.
6. Login with username created during installation or use root login.
7. It will start gnome initial setup.

26

8. Select language and press next.

9. Select keyboard type and press Next.

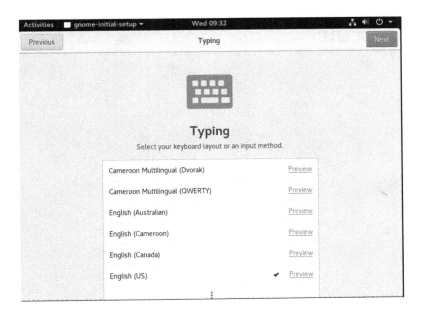

10. Set privacy settings.

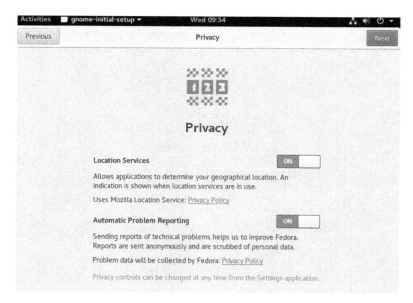

11. If you want to connect to cloud and online services, you can configure on this screen. Press skip if you do not want.

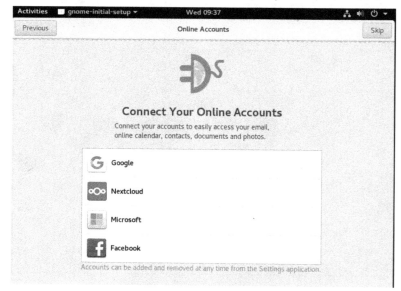

12. Now you are ready to use Fedora gnome desktop.

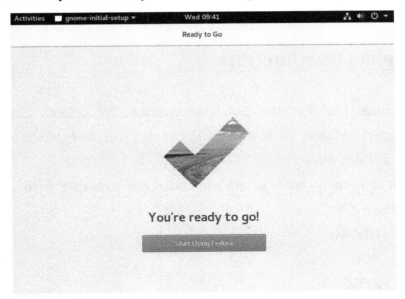

13. Press Start using Fedora it will open help/ Tutorials windows if you are new to Gnome 3 you can check this help otherwise close it to start using Fedora desktop.

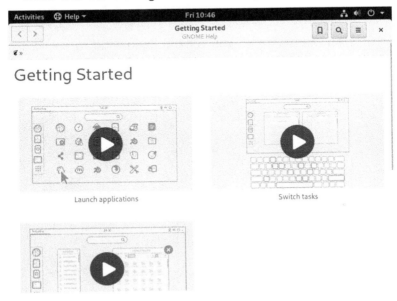

## Chapter 7

Graphics User Interface

Earlier we had installed Graphical desktop. By default, GNOME desktop is installed. Once desktop is installed you have choice to add more desktop environment.

There are many desktop environments are available from which prominent are:-

- GNOME
- KDE
- XFCE
- LXDE

In this chapter, we will explore GNOME desktop which is installed as default desktop

Graphical Login

When you start the machine, you will get login window

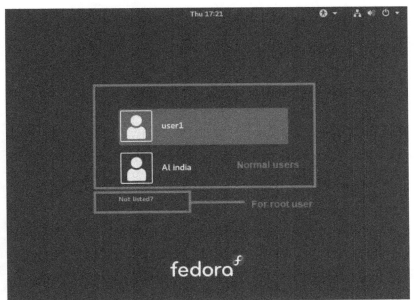

You press the user's icon to login as normal user. To login as root user, you select **Not listed?** from the graphical login screen. Once text box for login name appears type **root** and press **[Enter]**, type the root password that you selected during installation at the password prompt, and press **[Enter]**.

Virtual Console Login

When install Linux with Graphical desktop, usually you get six virtual consoles provide a text terminal with a login prompt to Linux shell. The graphical X Window System starts in the first virtual console. User switches between them with the key combination Alt plus a function key – for example Alt+F1 to access first virtual console. During installation, if you haven't selected graphical desktop you will see a login prompt similar to the following after booting your system

31

To log in from the console, type username at the login prompt, press Enter, then type the password and press Enter.

GNOME terminal

Gnome terminal is terminal emulator for gnome desktop environment. Terminal allows to you give command to your Fedora machine. By default you gets the **>** prompt if you login as normal user and **#** prompt if you login as root. To change to # prompt from > you use **su** command and password of root. To open Gnome Terminal Applications > Utilities > Terminal or Activities > write terminal in search bar and click on terminal icon

Commands

Ctrl +a	Moves the cursor to the beginning of the command prompt
Ctrl + e	Moves the cursor to the end of the command prompt
Ctrl + u	Clear the current line
Middle mouse button click	Paste the highlighted text
Tab	Completes the command
Up / Down Keys	Show history of commands
Ctrl +c	Terminate the current process
Ctrl + z	Suspends the foreground process

Disk Utility

To open disk utility press **Activities** in search bar write disks and click icon

With graphical disk utility you can

- Create / Delete / Edit partition
- Mount / Unmount file system
- Format volume to required File System Type
- Check File System
- Edit File system label
- Format drive
- Check benchmarks

From left pan select the required device then you can do operation on the device.

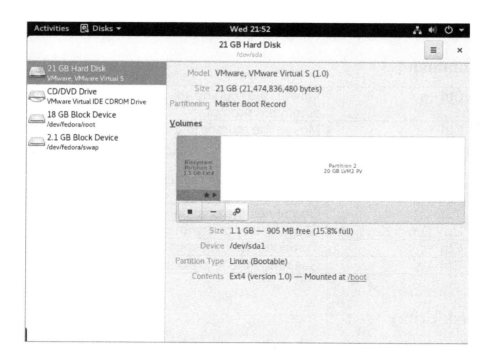

## Chapter 8

Network

Network is group of two or more computers connected together. Network allows interconnection between different machines. You require network card on each computer to connect. Every network card has physical address known as **M**edia **A**ccess **C**ontrol address (MAC address). MAC address works on layer 2 of OSI model. Manufacturer of network interface card assigns MAC addresses to network cards. As network card can go faulty and needs replacement, with replacement of network card the MAC address will also change. To overcome this problem we assign IP address to network card, which works on layer 3 of OSI model. As IP address are still numeric value it is difficult to remember more over there is possibility of IP address may change in case of dynamic IPs. To make life easy for humans we use **hostname,** which nothing but name of computers.

Just to give an idea about OSI model and list of applications and devices with their respective layers, a chart is given bellow.

Seven layer of OSI and TCP Mapping

OSI Model	TCP Model	Application	Address	Devices
7:Application layer	Application Layer	HTTP / Telnet / SSH	Applications DNS, DHCP.ntp,HTTP,	
6:Presentation layer		SSL / MIME		
5: Session layer		Sockets and Remote Procedure Call (RPC)		
4: Transport layer	Transport layer	Transmission Control Protocol (TCP)	TCP/UDP	Gateway
3: Network layer	Internet layer	Internet Protocol (IP)	IP4, IP6, IPX, ICMP	Router, firewall Layer 3 switch
2: Data link layer	Network Access Layer	Ethernet / Frame Relay	MAC address, ARP	Bridge Layer 2 switch
1: Physical layer		IEEE 802.x	Ethernet	HUB

Commands to check network configuration

After fresh installation, it is good idea to check the network configuration. As a best practice note down this configuration

Show IP address

```
# ip addr show
```
Or
```
# ifconfig -a
```

Show Link status

```
# ip link show
```

Show routing table

```
# ip route
```

Or

```
# netstat -rn
```

Check and change hostname

Show hostname

```
# hostname
```

Change hostname

Whenever you want to change hostname, you have to change it in two steps

1. Change hostname using command **hostnamectl**
2. Next change entry in /etc/hosts

1. Give hostnamectl command status to check the current

```
# hostnamectl status
   Static hostname: fedora1
        Icon name: computer
          Chassis: n/a
       Machine ID: 98c0429d893c48b88fba101f95aa70ca
          Boot ID: 864f0f4e99cd4442b4f388a15a7fc132
```

Or

```
# hostname
```

2. Change the hostname

```
# hostnamectl set-hostname fedora1
```

3. Next step is to change **/etc/hosts** file

```
127.0.0.1 fedora1 localhost.localdomain localhost
```

Setting Up the DNS Name Resolution

Whenever you write hostname instead of IP address to ping or to connect Linux host. You have multiple option to resolve hostname to IP address.

- Local file i.e. /etc/hosts
- DNS server
- NIS

/etc/hosts

Using local file **/etc/hosts** for hostname to IP address mapping provides ability to store list of hostname to their respective IP address you don't require to look for DNS server. It is also useful if you are connecting to limited servers due scope or security reason. You do not have to depend on DNS server.

Format

IP_address   hostname aliases

Example

```
127.0.0.1              fedora1 localhost
::1                    fedora1 localhost
192.168.228.129        fedora1
```

Using Domain Name Server for name resolution

/etc/resolv.conf

To resolve hostnames to IP addresses system reads a file called **resolv.conf**. You need to put your DNS server IP addresses in this file. Generally, you need one name server, but you can include up to three if you want redundancy.

If the first one on the list is not responding, system tries to resolve against the next one on the list, and so on.

Edit **/etc/resolv.conf** to add list of name servers, like this:

```
nameserver 8.8.8.8
nameserver 8.8.8.9
nameserver 1.2.3.6
```

Changing order for hostname resolution

/etc/nsswitch.conf

If hosts file and DNS configuration is there in **resolv.conf** in your server, Whenever you do hostname resolution the system looks for local file (**/etc/hosts**) for entry of hostname and respective IP address. If there is no entry, it looks for **/etc/resolv.conf** file for DNS configuration. If there is no DNS configuration also then it will check for NIS configuration. However, you can change this behavior by changing order in **/etc/nsswitch.conf** file.

```
vi /etc/nsswitch.conf
```

```
#hosts:      db files nisplus nis dns
hosts:       files dns
```

In this example search sequence is first files means **/etc/hosts** then DNS server.

Modifying Network configuration

In the earlier versions of Fedora, Network configuration was handled with files. However, in the recent versions of fedora it uses network manager. Network manager is dynamic network configuration and control daemon. It manages network devices and connections. The **ifcfg** configuration files which were used traditionally, still supported in fedora.

Network Manager configures

- IP address
- Static routes
- Network aliases
- VPN configuration
- DNS information

Check the status of networkmanager daemon

```
# systemctl status NetworkManager
```

Start Networkmanager if it is not working

```
# systemctl start NetworkManager
```

Enable it to start automatically with system start (Most of the time it is not requires as networkmanager is configured by default to start automatically)

```
# systemctl enable NetworkManager
```

Changing IP Address using Graphical interface

If static IP address is configured in your system or want to change dynamic IP to static IP address following steps are there

1. Login as root

2. Click Network manager icon, Select Connection and select Wired settings

3. Select click setting icon is small gear icon

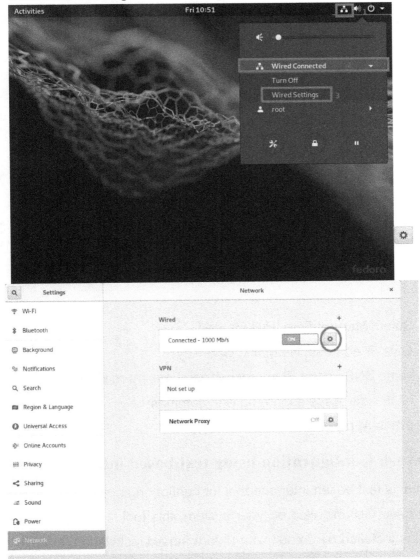

4. Select IPv4 settings

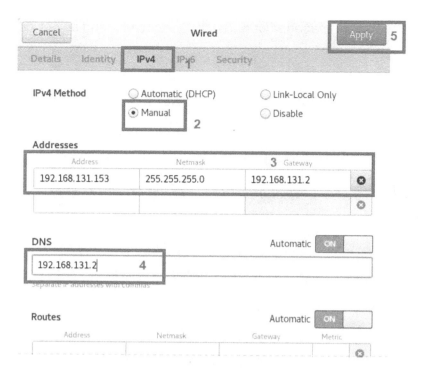

2. Select **Manual** from IPv4 Method
3. Give IP address, NetMask, Gateway
4. Write DNS server IP address. If you have more than one DNS give all IP addresses separated with commas
5. Press Apply

Network Configuration using text based interface nmtui

Nmtui is text based interface tool for configuring networking. If you do not have GUI installed on your system, this tool is very helpful. This tool is installed by default with fedora server installation. In case it is not there you can install it. To move around in this tool you use TAB, ARROW keys on the keyboard. For selecting item use SPACEBAR.

```
# dnf install NetworkManager-tui
```

To start nmtui

```
# nmtui
```

Commands

Edit the connection setting

Syntax

```
nmtui edit connection_name
```

Example

```
# nmtui edit 'Wired connection 1'
```

Connect the disconnected connection

Syntax

```
nmtui connect connection_name
```

Example

```
# nmtui connect 'Wired connection 1'
```

Change hostname using nmtui

Syntax

```
nmtui hostname new_hostname
```

Example

```
# nmtui hostname fedora21
```

Modifying IP address using NMTUI

Start nmtui

```
# nmtui
```

1. Select **Edit a connection**

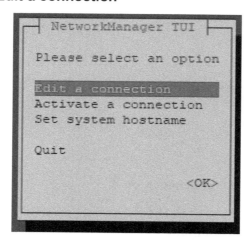

2. Select the connection profile from the list and press **Edit**

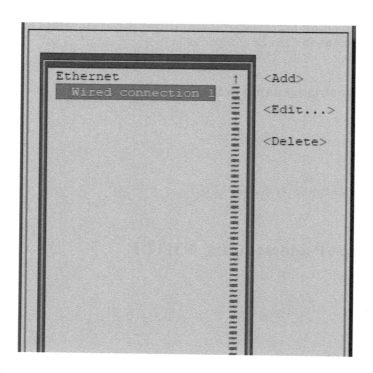

3. From the next screen press SPACE BAR key on IPv4 configuration to get popup menu. Select **Manual** to set static IP address.

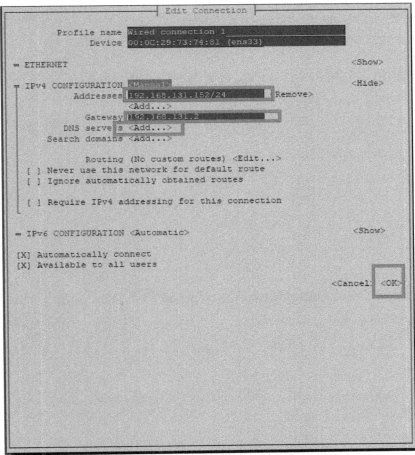

4. Give Address with Netmask in next column.

5. Write gateway and DNS in respective fields and press **OK**

6. Press ESC key to come out form NMTUI

Modifying network configuration using configuration files

If you do not have Graphical desktop and you love to work on configuration files, you can still use configuration files to control networking. In this example, I will explain how to change IP address of host using configuration files.

Changing IP address using configuration files

1. Check current setting

```
# ip addr show
```

2. Check current devices

```
[root@fedora2]# nmcli d
DEVICE  TYPE      STATE       CONNECTION
ens33   ethernet  connected   ens33
lo      loopback  unmanaged   --
```

3. Edit **/etc/sysconfig/network-scripts/ifcfg-***. Where **ifcfg-*** file is device file you just checked in last command. The command output shows **ens33** as device name then the file name will be **ifcfg-ens33**

```
# vi /etc/sysconfig/network-scripts/ifcfg-ens33
```

4. Change **/etc/sysconfig/network-scripts/ifcfg-ens33** file depending on where you have static IP address or you are using DHCP

Static	DHCP
DEVICE=eth0 BOOTPROTO=static IPADDR =192.168.0.132 NETMASK=255.255.255.0	DEVICE=eth0 BOOTPROTO=dhcp

GATEWAY=192.168.0.1 ONBOOT=yes	

5. Restart network services

```
# systemctl restart network
```

Adding static route using configuration file

To change static routes or to add new routes do the following

1. Check current routing table

```
# netstat -rn
```

or

```
# route -n
```

or

```
# ip route show
```

2. Edit /etc/sysconfig/network-scripts/route-interfacefile and add X.X.X.X/X via Y.Y.Y.Y dev interface Where X.X.X.X is IP address or network and Y.Y.Y.Y is gateway used by X.X.X.X

```
# vi /etc/sysconfig/network-scripts/route-ens33
```

Example

```
10.0.0.0/8 via 192.168.1.1
```

3. Restart network services

```
# systemctl restart network
```

4. Check the routing table again

```
# route -n
```

5. Ping the destination address

```
# ping 10.0.0.2
```

Changing DNS server using configuration file

Edit /etc/resolv.conf

```
search example.com        // give own FQDN
nameserver 8.8.8.8        // IPaddress of first DNS
nameserver 8.8.4.4        // IPaddress of Second DNS
```

Managing network interface

Bring down Ethernet interface

Syntax

```
Ifdown interface_name
```

Example

```
# ifdown ens33
```

Bring up Ethernet interface

Syntax

```
Ifup interface_name
```

Example

```
# ifup ens33
```

Important Network Commands

Task	Command
Check connectivity between two system	ping *IP_address* Example ping 10.1.1.2
Check IP address configuration	ifconfig -a or ip addr show
Check configuration of network card	cat /etc/sysconfig/network-scripts/ifcfg-*
Check routing table	ip route show
Querying DNS	dig
Local file to resolve hosts to IP address	/etc/hosts
DNS server configuration file	/etc/resolv.conf

## Chapter 9

Managing local users and groups

As Linux is a multi-user operating system, it allows multiple users on different computers to access a single system. As a system administrator you required to perform users and group management, which include add, modify remove users and groups according to policy of the organization the server belongs to.

User and group

A **user** is anyone who uses a computer. Users on Linux machine are ether people or accounts. The users are further logically grouped together in **groups**. Group is logical entity to organize users together based on their properties it can be either same department, same place or same work.

User Management Using GUI

Press the Window key to enter the Activities Overview, type Users and then press Enter. The Users settings tool appears.

Add User

Press Add user

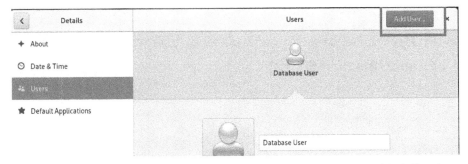

Once you click Add user button it presents new screen with following

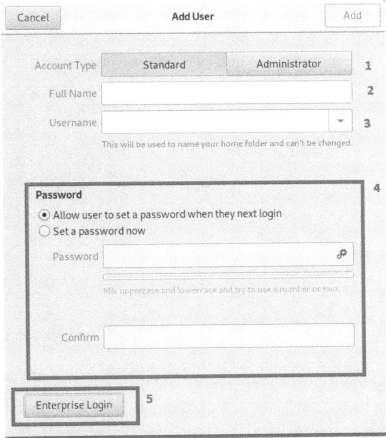

1. **Account type** Whether you want user to perform administrative tasks or not. It has two option Standard / Administrator.

2. **Full name** Full name of User or Description of user like David Arnold or Database User.

3. Username
4. **Password** Set password now or set by user on first login.
5. **Enterprise Login** For single sign on your machine and same time Active Directory or IPA domain.

Modify User

In the modify screen you can modify all details of user which you entered at time of creation except the name of user.

Open users, Select the user. Here you can change the users Full name, Account type password, auto login and check user last login

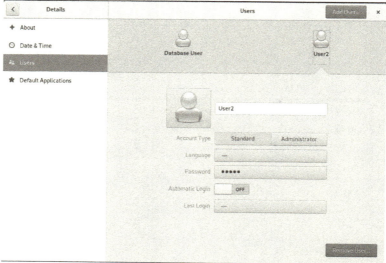

detail.

Remove User

Select the user on the users screen and press remove user. It will show popup which shows three option **Delete files** to delete the home directory and all files of the user. **Keep files** to leave the home directory as it is. **Cancel** to cancel this remove operation.

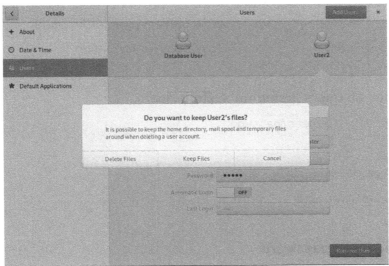

You must have noticed that user management screen of Gnome does not show root user and there is no screen for group management also. I don't know whether it is bug or "new feature ☺".

User Management Using Command Line

Add User

```
# useradd username
```

Now set the password

```
# passwd username
```

Delete user

```
# userdel username
```

Modify user

```
# usermod -c "database user" username
```

Display information about user

```
# id                 show current user information
# id username        Show users information
```

Display all users including system users

```
# cut -d: -f1 /etc/passwd
```

Change password for other user

```
# passwd username
```

Change own password

```
# passwd
```

List password expiry information

```
# chage -l username
```

Disable password expiration for user

```
# chage -I -1 -m 0 -M 99999 -E -1 username
```

Force user to change password at next login

```
# chage -d 0 user1
```

Lock user

```
# usermod -L user1
```

Unlock user

```
# usermod –U user1
```

UID

Unique User ID called as **UID**. UID is for every user exist on system. the range for UID is fixed for root and other users.

UID Range

User	UID
root	0
System user	1 – 999
Regular users	1000 +

Groups

Every user we create belongs to at least one group. All groups have unique group ID known as GID. **/etc/groups** file contains list of all available groups and entry of all member users of respective groups. There are two type of groups

- primary group
- secondary group

Primary group

This is the group applied when user logins and used by default when you create new files and directories. It is normally same name as username. Users primary group ID is written in **/etc/passwd** file for respective users in the third field.

Secondary Group

These are groups you are a member other than your primary group.

/etc/group

```
groupname:shadow password:GID:list of users in group
```

Example

```
science:x:1003:class1,class2
```

Changing primary group

```
# usermod -g data1 user1
```

Changing secondary group

```
# usermod -G data2 user1
```

Add new group

```
# groupadd groupname
```

Delete group

```
# groupdel groupname
```

/etc/passwd

Stores users information

Format

```
username:x:UID:GID:Full_user_name:home_directory:shellaccount
```

Username   up to 8 characters. Case-sensitive

x   Passwords are stored in the ``/etc/shadow" file.

UID   User ID

GID   Group ID

shell account Often set to **"/bin/bash"** to provide access to the bash shell, but it can be other shell like c shell, korn shell etc.

Example

```
root:x:0:0:root:/root:/bin/bash
```

/etc/shadow

Stores actual password in encrypted format

Format

```
username:password:last_password_change:minimum
```

Username up to 8 characters. Case-sensitive, usually all lowercase. A direct match to the username in the /etc/passwd file.

Password 13 character encrypted. A blank entry (eg. ::) indicates a password is not required to log in (usually a bad idea), and a " * " entry (eg. :*:) indicates the account has been disabled.

last_password_change The number of days (since January 1, 1970) since the password was last changed.

Minimum: The number of days before password may be changed (0 indicates it may be changed at any time)

Maximum: The number of days after which password must be changed (99999 indicates user can keep his or her password unchanged for many, many years)

Warn : The number of days to warn user of an expiring password (7 for a full week)

Inactive: The number of days after password expires that account is disabled

Expire: The number of days since January 1, 1970 that an account has been disabled

Example

```
root:$6$YtTXd..cW9GYuWT9sNwX07B3i.:17201:0:99999:7:::
```

## Chapter 10

NFS Network File System

NFS is file sharing file system, which works on server client basis. Server's shared file systems are mounted on client. Four version of NFS are there:-

1. NFS V1
2. NFS V2
3. NFS V3
4. NFS V4

Where NFS V3 and NFS V4 are more recent version of NFS, V3 is safer and asynchronous works on UDP protocol while V4 has added advantage of working through firewall and works on TCP.

/etc/exports

This file exists on the NFS server. This is configuration file used to export file system on server to clients. To export any file system, the entry should be added to this file.

To export file system without /etc/exports manually.

```
# exportfs -i /user1
```

To unexport all exported file system

```
# exportfs -ua
```

Configure NFS on the server

1. Install packages

```
# dnf install nfs-utils
# dnf install rpcbind
```

2. Start the services

```
# systemctl start rpcbind
# systemctl start nfs-server
```

3. Make service start on next reboot

```
# systemctl enable rpcbind
# systemctl enable nfs-server
```

4. Edit /etc/exports file to add filesystem you want to share to clients format of that is :-

```
mountpoint    [host][permissions/options]
```

   where

   mountpoint is file systems you want export

   host is optional the client you want to give access the file systems

   permissions is optional it can be **ro** read only ,**rw** read write

   insecure, sync changes written before command finished.

5. Export file system

```
# exportfs -a
```

6. See the file system exported

```
# showmount -e
```

7. Configure firewall to allow NFS server to clients

```
firewall-cmd --permanent --add-service mountd
firewall-cmd --permanent --add-service rpc-bind
firewall-cmd --permanent --add-service nfs
firewall-cmd --reload
```

8. On client

```
# showmount -e server IP address / hostname
# mount -t nfs 192.168.0.1:/userfs /newmnt
```

## Chapter 11

Process and threads

Every task done by Linux OS has process associated with it. Process has priority based on the context switches on them.

Each process provide resources needed to execute the program

Each process starts with single thread known as primary thread. Process can have multiple threads.

Process runs in foreground and background

Commands

Command	Description
bg	Sends job to Background
fg	Bring job to foreground
jobs	Show current jobs
kill	Stops the process
ps	Show the process information
&	if command ends with the & the shell execute the command in background and shell will not wait for finish Example gcalctool &

Bring command to foreground

```
# fg
ctrl + c
```

Check the running jobs

```
# jobs
```

List the current running process

```
# ps -ef |grep gcalctool
```

or

```
# ps aux
```

Kill the process forcefully

First check the process ID with **ps –ef** command then

```
# kill -9 <process -id >
```

Monitoring the process with ps command

ps command show the percentage of CPU & memory utilization of the process it is very useful if your machine is under performing. **ps** command gives you indication which process is hogging memory/CPU.

Process scheduling

Scheduler is part of kernel, which select process to run next. The purpose is to run the processes according to priorities. To set the priority of running process nice and renice command is used which decide how longer or smaller CPU time is given to process.

nice set the priority or niceness of new process.

renice adjust nice value of running process

niceness of -20 is highest priority and 19 is lowest priority. The default priority is 0

Example

```
# nice -n 19 cp -r /as /map
```

Commands show priorities of running processes

```
# ps -al
```

or

```
# top
```

To change the priority

```
# renice -n 10 <pid>
```

Note: You need root privilege to change to higher priority.

## Chapter 12

Automating tasks

Fedora has utilities to automate the task which system administrator do regularly or at specified time. Following are the main utilities

- cron
- at
- batch

Cron

cron is daemon that can be used to schedule the execution of recurring tasks according to time, day of month, day of week. it accepts machine to running continuously like server. If at time of schedule the system is down it will skip the task.

Configuration file

/etc/crontab

Command

Command	Description
crontab –l	List crontab entries
crontab –e	Edit crontab
crontab –r	Remove crontab

Format

```
minutes hours Day_of_month Month Day_of_week  Command
```

Where

Minutes   (from 0 to 59)

hours   (from 0 to 23)

day of month	(from 1 to 31)
month	(from 1 to 12)
day of week	(from 0 to 6) (0=Sunday)

To schedule a recurring task

1. Edit crontab by giving command **crontab –e.** It will open crontab file in vi environment. You can use vi command to save and exit.

2. Add entries at bottom of file press **i**

Suppose you want to run backup script every night at 11:30

```
30 23 * * *        /myscripts/backup.sh
```

3. Press [escape] and press : write **x** after that press [enter] to save the entry

Anacron

Anacorn is also to execute the scheduled tasks, unlike cron it is meant for laptop and pc users where machine is not up 24x 7.

Anacron remembers the scheduled jobs if the system is not running at the time when the job is scheduled. The job is then executed as soon as the system is up. However, Anacron can only run a job once a day

Just like how cron has **/etc/crontab**, anacron has **/etc/anacrontab**.

/etc/anacrontab following format.

```
period    delay    job-identifier    command
```

at and batch

crontab is used for recurring tasks but for one time tasks at specified time **at** and **batch** commands are used.

To run at command rpm must be installed and **atd** service must be running

Check Installation

```
# rpm -q at
```

Install at package

```
# dnf install at
```

Start service

```
# systemctl start atd
```

Start command

```
# at 4:00
at > ls
ctrl + d
```

Batch command executes one time task when system average load decreases bellow 0.8

```
# at
at > ls
ctrl + d
```

Display list of pending jobs

```
atq
```

## Chapter 13

Log management

Log files are very useful in troubleshooting and auditing system for unauthorized system access.

Using GUI to view log files

To view log files in GUI, use the GNOME Logs application. Logs application is not installed by default, if it is not there you can install it. Press the Windows Button and type Logs.

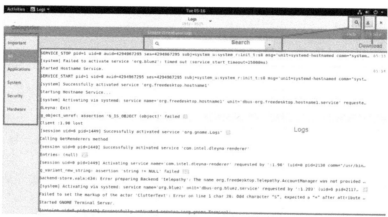

When you open logs application you will see the screen on the left side it shows categories. Left Pan shows logs. You have option to download the log in a file and search the log file for particular string or error.

Rysylogd

In Fedora some logs are controlled by **rsyslogd** daemon. It is enhanced replacement of **sysklogd**. It offers high-performance, great security features, modular design and support for transportation via the TCP or UDP protocols.

rsyslogd reads the file **/etc/rsyslog.conf. rsyslogd** can be configured vai **rsyslog.conf** file. List of log files maintained by **rsyslogd** can be found in the rsyslog.conf configuration file. Log files are usually located in the /var/log/ directory.

Install

```
# dnf install rsyslog
```

Configuration file

/etc/rsyslog.conf

Sample rsyslog.conf

```
[root@ fedora1 etc]# cat rsyslog.conf
# rsyslog v5 configuration file

# For more information see /usr/share/doc/rsyslog-*/rsyslog_conf.html
#       If      you      experience      problems,      see
http://www.rsyslog.com/doc/troubleshoot.html


#### MODULES ####

$ModLoad imuxsock # provides support for local system logging (e.g. via
logger command)
$ModLoad imklog   # provides kernel logging support (previously done by
rklogd)
#$ModLoad immark  # provides --MARK-- message capability

# Provides UDP syslog reception
#$ModLoad imudp
#$UDPServerRun 514

# Provides TCP syslog reception
#$ModLoad imtcp
#$InputTCPServerRun 514
```

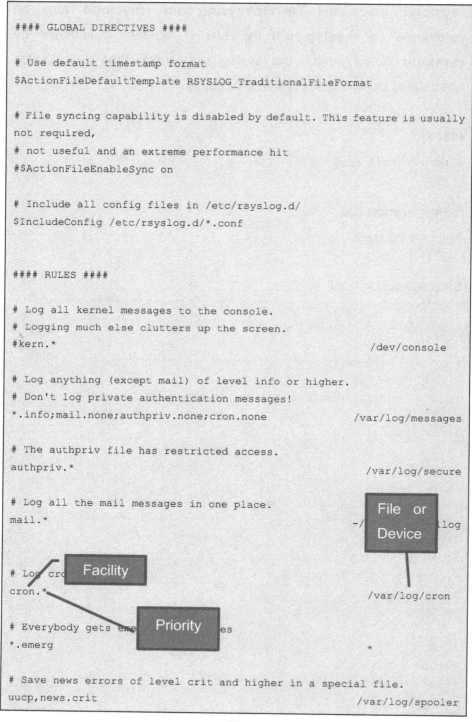

```
#### GLOBAL DIRECTIVES ####


# Use default timestamp format
$ActionFileDefaultTemplate RSYSLOG_TraditionalFileFormat

# File syncing capability is disabled by default. This feature is usually
not required,
# not useful and an extreme performance hit
#$ActionFileEnableSync on

# Include all config files in /etc/rsyslog.d/
$IncludeConfig /etc/rsyslog.d/*.conf



#### RULES ####

# Log all kernel messages to the console.
# Logging much else clutters up the screen.
#kern.*                                              /dev/console

# Log anything (except mail) of level info or higher.
# Don't log private authentication messages!
*.info;mail.none;authpriv.none;cron.none            /var/log/messages

# The authpriv file has restricted access.
authpriv.*                                           /var/log/secure

# Log all the mail messages in one place.
mail.*                                            -/                    log

# Log cron                                             /var/log/cron
cron.*

# Everybody gets emerg           es
*.emerg                                                       *

# Save news errors of level crit and higher in a special file.
uucp,news.crit                                       /var/log/spooler
```

```
# Save boot messages also to boot.log
local7.*                                              /var/log/boot.log
```

Log filtering

There is too much logging happens in the system if it is not filtered it become almost impossible to use logs. To filter the logs we use **/etc/rsyslog.conf** file. It has two parameter facility and priority separated with dot(.). Facility is name of process for which you want to log and priority specify level of log like debug, info, notice, warning, err, crit , alert, emerg you want to keep.

Example

```
# The authpriv file has restricted access.
authpriv.*                                            /var/log/secure

# Log all the mail messages in one place.
mail.*                                                          _
/var/log/maillog
```

In the example where **authpriv** and **mail** is facility and * is priority mean all logs.

journald

Logs can also be managed by the **journald** daemon, a component of **systemd**. It's a centralized location for all messages logged by different components in a systemd-enabled Linux system. This includes kernel and boot messages, initial RAM disk, messages coming from syslog or different services, it indexes them and makes this available to the user. The native journal file format, improves searching it stores Meta data with time stamp and user's ID. Log files produced by journald are not persistent, log files are stored only in memory or a small ring-buffer in the **/run/log/journal/** directory. The amount of logged data depends on free memory, logs gets rotated periodically.

By default, these two logging tools i.e. **rsyslogd** and **journald** coexist on your system

Viewing log with journalctl

To view log

```
# journalctl
```

To view full meta data about all entries

```
# journalctl -o verbose
```

Live view of logs

```
# journalctl -f
```

Filtering by Priority

Syntax

```
# journalctl -p priority
```

Example

Filtering by error

```
# journalctl -p err
```

View all alerts in log

```
# journalctl -p alert
```

To view log entries only form the current boot

```
# journalctl -b
```

To make logs persistent

```
# mkdir -p /var/log/journal
```

Then, restart journald to apply the change:

```
# systemctl restart systemd-journald
```

Rotating logs

logrotate

Logs needs rotation to avoid filling of file systems and make log more manageable.

Once log file is rotated, it will be renamed with new file name. After certain time of rotation older log files will get deleted to save space.

logrotate package manages automatically rotating of log files according to configuration in **/etc/logrotate.conf**

logwatch

logwatch is program to analyze and reporting short digest via mail.

Can   be   configured   vai **/usr/share/logwatch/default.conf/logwatch.conf** configuration file.

Install

```
#dnf install logwatch
```

Configure

Setting configuration file

/usr/share/logwatch/default.conf/logwatch.conf.

The email address to which daily digest(report) are sent

MailTo =root

Example

```
# Default person to mail reports to.  Can be a local account or
a
# complete email address.  Variable Print should be set to No
to
# enable mail feature.
MailTo = root
```

## Chapter 14

Software management

Linux is collection of packages. If you are using any OS you have to manage software. Some time you have to add of software other time you have to remove. Once new update of software is available you have to update it also. Installing, removing and updating software is very difficult using source files. When you are using source files to install package first you compile and then install it. Moreover, before install you have to fulfill its dependencies also.

To make the life easy for Linux users the most of the distributions uses package manager which handles downloading required packages from internet or local device and installing software with one command. These package managers also download and install dependencies if any is required. Like other Linux distributions which may have their own commands for package management fedora uses **dnf** command for software management. When you issue dnf command with option and required package name it download the package from internet or local software warehouse known as **repository**. It also makes sure all required software that is needed to run this software also gets installed.

Repository

Repository is collection of software for Linux, ether present locally or remotely. The repository can be used to install additional software or to update the current software. The location for repositories configuration files is **/etc/yum.repos.d/** directory.

Display all enabled repositories

```
# dnf repolist
```

Display all repositories enabled and disabled

```
# dnf repolist all
```

DNF

The **dnf** is new package manager for fedora project Introduced in Fedora 18, it has been the default package manager since Fedora 22.

DNF or Dandified yum is the next generation version of **YUM**. DNF is command line tool for package management. DNF uses repository to fetch the correct version of a particular package compatible for your system. DNF allows automatic update of packages and dependency management. It allows automatically download of the packages and install them from repositories. Repository can be remote repository like internet site or local repository such as CDROM or directory. Not only repositories provided by fedora, you can also use third party repositories to install extra packages like open office, VLC etc.

DNF provides secure package management by enabling GPG (GNU privacy guard) signature verification. Which makes sure that only trusted packages are installed from repositories.

Configuration file of dnf is **/etc/dnf/dnf.conf**. You can also set repositories in this file, but it is recommended creating separate **.repo** file for each repository in **/etc/yum.repos.d** directory

To check the configuration of DNF

```
# dnf config-manager --dump
```

Commands

Package

Install package

Syntax

```
# dnf install -y package_name
```

Example

```
# dnf install -y firefox
```

Remove package

Syntax

```
# dnf remove package_name
```

Example

```
# dnf remove firefox
```

Check available updates

```
# dnf check-update
```

Update system using dnf

```
# dnf update
```

Check the file provided by which package

```
# dnf provides file-name
```

Example

```
# dnf remove firefox
```

Get help

```
# dnf help
```

list the installed and available software

```
# dnf list
```

search the package name with keyword

```
# dnf search keyword
```

Example

```
# dnf search firefox
```

Display information about the package

Syntax

```
# dnf info package_name
```

Example

```
# dnf info zip
```

Update all software provided by the repository

```
# dnf update
```

Clean the dnf cache

```
# dnf clean all
```

List dnf history

```
# dnf history list
```

Package group

Package group is group of software, which have same motive to install. It makes administrator's life easy by installing and downloading dependent software automatically. For example, you want to install backup client you give command **dnf group install 'Backup Client'**

List all package group available

```
# dnf group list
```

78

Install group package

Syntax

```
dnf group install package_name
```

Example

```
# dnf group install 'LibreOffice'
```

Remove group package

Syntax

```
dnf group remove package_name
```

Example

```
# dnf group remove 'Backup Client'
```

Information about group package

Syntax

```
# dnf group info package_name
```

Example

```
# dnf group info 'Network Servers'
```

Repository

To install additional package or update existing package you require repository. It is warehouse of all Linux software. **DNF** repository can hold **RPM** packages located locally like CDROM , directory on local disk or remotely like FTP, HTTP or HTTPS. The configuration files for name, location, status etc. of each repository is there in **/etc/yum.repos.d/** directory.

The configuration file present in the **/etc/yum.repos.d/** directory have following fields

Repository ID - Single word unique repository ID

Name - Name of the repository (example: name=CD_media)

Baseurl - URL to the repodata directory. You can use ftp://link, http://link, https://link if repository is located remotely and file://path if repository is located locally (example file:///mnt/ for mnt directory locally)

Enabled - Enable/Disable repository (example: enabled=1 to enable or enable=0 to disable)

Gpgcheck - Enable/disable GPG signature checking (example: gpgcheck=1)

Gpgkey - location of GPG key

Defining repository

1. Create file /etc/yum.repos.d/<name>.repo
2. Add following contents

```
[Repository_ID]
name=name_of_repository
baseurl=http://location
enabled=1
gpgcheck=0
```

Using DVD or local directory as repository

1. Mount the fedora installation ISO to a directory like /mnt, e.g.:

```
# mount -o loop fedora.iso /cdrom
```

2. If you use DVD media, you can mount like below.

```
# mount -o ro /dev/cdrom1 /cdrom
```

Where /dev/cdrom1 is DVDROM device you may have different one.

3. Create file name cdrom.repo in **/etc/yum.repos.d/** that should look like the following where /cdrom is directory where cdrom is mounted

```
[installmedia]
name=Fedora 29
baseurl=file:///cdrom/
gpgcheck=0
enabled=1
```

4. Clear the related caches by **dnf clean all**

```
# dnf clean all
```

5. Now check the repository

```
# dnf repolist all
```

Installing packages with RPM command

RPM

RPM stands for Red Hat Package Manager. RPM packages have .rpm extension. **rpm** command is used to manage software which include list, install, update and remove . RPM is usually used to install packages which has been downloaded locally. Unlike DNF, RPM does not install dependencies automatically. This means you have to install dependent software first before installing actual package.

Commands

Install

Syntax

```
rpm -ihv  package_name
```

Example

```
# rpm -ihv zip-3.0-23.fc29.x86_64.rpm
Preparing...
######################################### [100%]
   1:zip
######################################### [100%]
```

Update
Syntax

```
rpm -Uhv package_name
```

Example

```
# rpm -Uhv zip-3.0-23.fc29.x86_64.rpm
```

Remove
Syntax

```
rpm -ev package_name
```

Example

```
# rpm -ev zip
```

Query all installed packages
Syntax

```
rpm -qa
```

Display detailed information about package
Syntax

```
rpm -qi package_name
```

Example

```
[root@server1 z]# rpm -qi zip
Name      : zip
Version   : 3.0
```

```
Release      : 23.fc29
Architecture: x86_64
Install Date: Thu 15 Nov 2018 07:23:44 AM EST
Group        : Applications/Archiving
Size         : 837661
License      : BSD
Signature    : RSA/SHA256, Sun 15 Jul 2018 11:09:03 PM EDT,
Key ID a20aa56b429476b4
Source RPM   : zip-3.0-23.fc29.src.rpm
Build Date   : Sun 15 Jul 2018 03:15:23 PM EDT
Build Host   : buildhw-09.phx2.fedoraproject.org
Relocations  : (not relocatable)
Packager     : Fedora Project
Vendor       : Fedora Project
URL          : http://www.info-zip.org/Zip.html
Bug URL      : https://bugz.fedoraproject.org/zip
Summary      : A file compression and packaging utility
compatible with PKZIP
Description :
The zip program is a compression and file packaging utility.
Zip is
analogous to a combination of the UNIX tar and compress
commands and
is compatible with PKZIP
…..
```

Find the file belongs to which package

Syntax

```
rpm -qf  path_to_the_file
```

Example

```
# rpm -qf /etc/hosts
```

```
setup-2.12.1-1.fc29.noarch
```

Find out all dependences

Syntax

```
rpm -qpR package_name
```

Example

```
# rpm -qpR zip-3.0-20.fc29.x86_64.rpm
libbz2.so.1()(64bit)
libc.so.6()(64bit)
libc.so.6(GLIBC_2.14)(64bit)
libc.so.6(GLIBC_2.2.5)(64bit)
libc.so.6(GLIBC_2.3)(64bit)
libc.so.6(GLIBC_2.3.4)(64bit)
libc.so.6(GLIBC_2.4)(64bit)
libc.so.6(GLIBC_2.7)(64bit)
rpmlib(CompressedFileNames) <= 3.0.4-1
rpmlib(FileDigests) <= 4.6.0-1
rpmlib(PayloadFilesHavePrefix) <= 4.0-1
rpmlib(PayloadIsXz) <= 5.2-1
rtld(GNU_HASH)
unzip
```

## Chapter 15

Backup and Restore

Backup of your computer data is always important to prevent data loss. Backup saves you in case of data loss. There are many reasons for data loss like hard disk failure ,OS failure, virus, malware or due to human error. Before taking actual backup you should try to answer three W's : what, when and where

What

In my experience as an administrator if you ask any user what part of data is important for backup, the simple, answer will be whole data. As an administrator, you should understand it is ideal to take backup of whole system daily but in practical, you require large device which can accommodate the whole data. Moreover taking backup also takes time. Suppose if you are taking backup of server which is online and you want to take backup of whole system, it may take hours to finish. In this case, by the time you are on verge of finishing the backup half the data has already changed. Therefore, data insistency arises. Best way to take consistent data backup is to stop the whole system and then take backup but if your backup window is large then it is very difficult to get down time in production systems. The solution for this problem is to segregate the data in to two or more parts, data which is changing regularly and the data which changes once while. The best example of that in production you have software binaries which changes very rarely and data files which gets updated regularly. You

85

can take backup of whole system monthly or quarterly and take backup of data files daily.

Where

Next question is where you want to keep backup. There two part of this question first part is device on which you want to take backup. It can be external hard disk, tape drive, DVD or even USB drive. The second part of question is the location where you want to physically keep the backup media. It can be stored at same location means onsite or offsite means at remote location. The benefit of storing at same location is easy and quick availability in case of loss of data but when there is total loss of site in case of natural disasters like flood and hurricane or in case fire offsite backup is more useful. According to the best practices, you should follow 3-2-1 plan. In this, you keep three backup copies of your data two copies onsite and third copy offsite. If condition arises in which you require backup copy to restore data you have two good copies of data onsite and in case of total disaster remote copy is there.

When

Next question, when backup has be done? It all depends on your business needs. Frequency of data change and criticality of data. Next thing is type of system it can be file server, data base server and desktop may have different windows of backup.

Backup type

Now you know the answer of three W's its time to understand backup more in depth. Backup is broadly of three types depending on how much of backup you are taking.

1. Full backup
2. Differential backup
3. Incremental backup

Full backup

As name suggest it is backup which contains all files. When you require to restore only one full backup is required.

Differential backup

A differential backup is cumulative backup of files, which have changed since last full backup. In case of restore only last full backup and last differential backup is required.

Incremental backup

Incremental backup backs up only the changed data since the last backup whether it is a full or incremental backup. Suppose you have taken full backup on Sunday and Monday you will take incremental backup which is changed files since Sunday and on Tuesday if you take incremental backup you will backup only files which has changed since last incremental backup i.e. Monday. But if you take differential backup on Tuesday it will take backup of all files which have changed since full backup i.e Sunday.

Tools for Backup and Restore

Tar

Use to create one archive file of multiple files. This file can be copied on tape, DVD or USB drive as a backup. You can also create compress file with adding option while creating achieve file.

Create tar

Syntax

```
tar cvf name_of_archive_file files_or_directory_to_archive
```

Where

c   create

v   verbose

f   file name types of achieve file

Example

```
# tar cvf abc.tar *
applications/
applications/preferred-mail-reader.desktop
applications/preferred-web-browser.desktop
gvfs-metadata/
# ls -la
total 96
drwxr-xr-x. 4 root root  4096 Feb 12 10:58 .
drwxr-xr-x. 3 root root  4096 Feb  4 12:46 ..
-rw-r-r--. 1 root root 81920 Feb 12 10:58 abc.tar
```

Create compressed tar file

You can compress the archive backup also using tar options. Tar provides two type of compression gzip and bzip.

Create gzip format tar file

```
# tar cvfz nameoftarfile.tar.gz name_of_files
```

Create bzip compressed format tar file

```
# tar cvfj nameoftarfile.tar.bz2 name_of_files
```

Extract

To restore the files taken backup with tar command

```
# tar xvf abc.tar
```

Where

x   extract

v   verbose

f   file name types of achieve file

gzip format

Syntax

```
tar xvfz filename
```

Example

```
# tar xvfz abc.tar.gz
```

bzip format

Syntax

```
tar xvfj filename
```

Example

```
# tar xvfj abc.tar.bz2
```

List

Tar command can be used with **t** option to show list of files/ folders it contains.

List the archived tar file

Syntax

```
tar tvf filename
```

Example

```
# tar tvf abc.tar
```

List gzip compressed tar file

Syntax

```
tar tzvf filename
```

Example

```
# tar tzvf abc.tar.gz
```

List bzip compressed tar file

Syntax

```
tar tjvf filename
```

Example

```
# tar tjvf abc.tar.bz2
```

CPIO

Cpio utility copies files from and to achieve. It is used for creating and extracting achieve file and for coping files from one place to another.

Creating achieve file of directory abc to /directory backup

```
# cd abc
# ls |cpio -ov > /backup/abc.cpio
```

Extract

```
# mkdir newbackup
# cd newbackup
# cpio idv < /backup/abc.cpio
```

Creating archive from list of specific files.

Example :- archieve all log files

```
# find . -iname *.log -print|cpio -ov > /backup/selog.cpio
```

Using cpio to create tar file

```
# ls|cpio -ovH tar -F abc.tar
```

To extract tar file using cpio

```
# cpio -idv -F abc.tar
```

## Chapter 16

Utilities and Commands

In this chapter we will discuss some of the common command utilities very useful in administration. Most of the commands discussed in chapter can be used on almost any flavor of Linux.

cp

Command to copy files

Syntax

```
cp <options> source destination
```

Example

```
cp /home/abc.txt /home1/
```

Copy all files in the directory recursively

```
cp -R /home/* /home1/
```

Prompt before any overwrite

```
# cp -i /home /home1
```

Copy all new files to the destination

```
# cp -u * /tmp
```

Forcefully copy files

```
# cp -f /tmp/abc.txt /backup/.
```

Copy without prompting to overwrite

```
# cp -n * t
```

scp

scp command is used to copy files form one host to other host in secured manner.

Copy files from local machine to remote machine

Syntax

```
scp filename remote_user@remotehost:/some/remote_diectory
```

Copy file from remote host to local host

Syntax

```
scp remote_user@remote.host:/some/remote_diectory/filename .
```

ls

Lists the Names of Files

Syntax

```
ls -<options>
```

Example

```
# ls -al
```
To list directories and files

cat

Displays a Text File

Syntax

```
cat filename
```

Example

```
# cat abc.conf
```

rm

Deletes a file, files or directory

Syntax

```
rm filename
```

Example

```
rm abc.conf
```

To delete abc directory recursively

```
rm -r abc
```

More

When you want to view a file that is longer than one screen, you can more utility. More is used for paging through text one screen full at a time.

Syntax

```
more filename
```

Example

```
# more /etc/hosts
```

less

Less is a program similar to more, but it allows backward movement in the file as well as forward movement.

Syntax

```
less filename
```

Example

```
# less /etc/hosts
```

mv

mv command is used to move file form one location to other location. You can also use mv command to rename the file without moving it.

To move file

Syntax

```
mv filename destination_directory
```

Example

```
mv a.txt /tmp/.
```

It will move a.txt file from current directory to /tmp directory

To rename

Syntax

```
mv filename newfilename
```

Example

```
mv a.txt b.txt
```

grep

Searches for a String from one or more files. Display each line which has string.

Syntax

```
grep string file
```

Example

```
# grep '127.0.0.1' /etc/hosts
```

head

Print the first 10 lines of file to standard output. You can also specify how many line it will show.

Syntax

```
head option file
```
Example

```
# head -20 /etc/mime.types
```

it will show first 20 lines of mime.types file

tail

Print the last 10 lines of file to standard output. You can also specify how many line it will show.

Syntax

```
tail option file
```

Example

```
# tail -20 /var/log/logfile
```

it will show last 20 lines

Use tail to monitor file continuously

```
# tail -f /var/log/logfile
```

It will show end of growing file. **Ctrl +c** to interrupt

diff

Compares Two Files.

Syntax

```
diff First_file   Second_file
```

Example

```
# diff abc.txt bbc.txt
```

file

Determine file type

Syntax

```
file file_name
```

Example

```
# file bbc.txt
```

echo

Display text

Syntax

echo text

Example

```
# echo hello
```

Date

Print or change the system data and time.

Syntax

```
date
```

Example

```
# date                         To check date
```

```
# date -s "24 feb 2017 19:00"        To set date
```

timedatectl

To display the current date and time along with detailed information

```
[root@fedora2 etc]# timedatectl
      Local time: Fri 2017-03-31 16:46:21 IST
  Universal time: Fri 2017-03-31 11:16:21 UTC
        RTC time: Fri 2017-03-31 11:16:21
       Time zone: Asia/Kolkata (IST, +0530)
 Network time on: yes
 NTP synchronized: yes
 RTC in local TZ: no
```

Change time

Syntax

```
timedatectl set-time HH:MM:SS
```

Example

```
timedatectl set-time 23:12:00
```

Change current date

```
# timedatectl set-time YYYY-MM-DD
```

Example

```
# timedatectl set-time '2013-06-02 23:26:00'
```

Synchronizing the Clock with a Remote Server

Syntax

```
# timedatectl set-ntp Boolean
```

Example

```
# timedatectl set-ntp yes
```

## Chapter 17

Piping and Redirection

Piping and redirection is important feature of Linux. Piping and redirection allows you change direction of input and output of command.

Sending output to file (>)

Normally, we will get our output on the screen, but if we wish to save it into a file the greater than operator (>) is used to send the standard out to file.

Example

```
# ls > abc.txt
```

Sending input from file (<)

If we use the less than operator (<) then we can read data from file and feed it into the program via it's STDIN stream.

Example

```
# wc -l < abc.txt
```

Piping (|)

For sending data from one program to another we use pipe (|)

```
# ls | head -10
```

## Chapter 18

Compression utilities

There are mainly three utilities to zip the files

Compression	Extension	Uncompress
bzip2	bz2	bunzip2
Gzip	gz	gunzip
Zip	zip	unzip

Compress

bzip2 format

Syntax

```
bzip2 file_to_backups
```

Example

```
# bzip2 *
```

gzip format

Syntax

```
gzip file_to_backups
```

Example

```
# gzip abc
```

zip format

Syntax

```
zip zipfile.zip file_to_backups
```

Example

```
# zip abc.zip *
```

Uncompress

bzip2 format

Syntax

```
bunzip2 filename
```

Example

```
# bunzip2 abc.bz2
```

gzip format

Syntax

```
gunzip filename
```

Example

```
# gunzip abc.gz
```

zip format

Syntax

```
unzip filename
```

Example

```
# unzip abc.zip
```

## Chapter 19

Managing services

Daemons

Daemons are processes, which run in the background and not interactively. Daemons perform some predefined actions at predefined time. Generally, daemons start at bootup and remain till shutdown. Mostly daemons name ends with **d**.

Services

Earlier versions of Fedora there used be scripts located in the /etc/rc.d/init.d/ directory and where used to control state of service and daemons.

In recent Fedora , these init scripts have been replaced with service units, service units resides in **/etc/systemd/system/** directory. Service units end with the .service file extension **systemctl** command is used to view, start, stop, restart, enable, or disable system services.

Service can start at boot time using **systemctl enable name.service** command

Service Status Management

Starts a service	systemctl start name.service Example systemctl start iscsi.service
Stops a service	systemctl stop name.service Example systemctl stop iscsi.service
Restarts a service	systemctl restart name.service Example systemctl restart iscsi.service

Restarts a service only if it is running.	systemctl try-restart name.service Example systemctl try-restart iscsi.service
Reloads configuration	systemctl reload *name*.service Example systemctl reload iscsi.service
Checks if a service is running.	systemctl status *name*.service systemctl is-active *name*.service Example systemctl status iscsi.service
Displays the status of all service	systemctl list-units --type service --all or systemctl -at service

Enable and disable service at startup

Enable service	systemctl enable *name*.service Example systemctl enable iscsi.service
Disable service	systemctl disable *name*.service Example systemctl disable iscsi.service
To prevent service from starting dynamically or even manually unless unmasked	systemctl mask *name*.service Example systemctl mask iscsi.service
Check whether a service enabled or not	systemctl is-enabled *name*.service Example systemctl is-enabled iscsi.service
Lists all services and checks if they are enabled or not	systemctl list-unit-files --type service

Service unit information

When we give command **systemctl -status name.service**. it provides following information

Field Description

103

Field	Description
Loaded	Whether the service unit is loaded, the absolute path to the unit file, whether the unit is enabled.
Active	Running or not
Main PID	PID of the service
Process	Information about process
CGroup	information about Control Groups.

Example

```
# systemctl status abrt-ccpp.service
abrt-ccpp.service - Install ABRT coredump hook
    Loaded: loaded (/usr/lib/systemd/system/abrt-ccpp.service;
enabled)
    Active: active (exited) since Sat 2017-03-18 06:05:25 IST; 1h
7min ago
  Process: 1013 ExecStart=/usr/sbin/abrt-install-ccpp-hook install
(code=exited, status=0/SUCCESS)
 Main PID: 1013 (code=exited, status=0/SUCCESS)
   CGroup: /system.slice/abrt-ccpp.service
```

systemd Targets

Previous versions of Fedora use to implement run levels. Run level is state or mode of OS in which it will run. Each run level has certain number of services stopped or started providing control over behavior of machine. However, in recent Fedora versions it is replaced by **systemd targets** there were seven **Runlevels** replaced by corresponding **target units**

Run level	Description	Target unit
0	halt the machine	poweroff.target
1	single user mode	rescue.target
2	multiuser with command line no GUI	multiuser.target
3	multiuser with command line no GUI	multiuser.target
4	multiuser with command line no GUI	multiuser.target
5	multiuser with GUI	graphical.target
6	reboot	reboot.target

Commands

List currently loaded target

```
# systemctl list-units --type target
```

Change the target

Switch to multiuser

```
# systemctl isolate multi-user.target
```

Switch to GUI mode

```
# systemctl isolate graphical.target
```

Change default target

```
# systemctl set-default <name of target>.target
```

Viewing the Default Target

```
# systemctl get-default
```

Changing the Current Target

```
# systemctl isolate <name of target>.target
```

Managing services startup

To list all services and there status

```
# systemctl -at service
```

To list current setting of specific service

Syntax

```
systemctl status name.service
```

Example

```
# systemctl status httpd.service
```

Enabling service

Syntax

```
systemctl enable name.service
```

Example

```
# systemctl enable iscsi.service
```

To disable service

Syntax

```
systemctl disable name.service
```

Example

```
# systemctl disable iscsi.service
```

Managing the services status

Determine status of service whether it is running or not

Syntax

```
# systemctl status name.service
```

Example

```
# systemctl status httpd.service
```

Starting service

Syntax

```
# systemctl start name.service
```

Example

```
# systemctl start httpd.service
```

Stopping service

Syntax

```
# systemctl stop name.service
```

Example

```
# systemctl stop httpd.service
```

Restarting service

Syntax

```
# systemctl restart name.service
```

Example

```
# systemctl restart httpd.service
```

Install new service

Procedure to install new service

1. Install new service package

   ```
   # dnf install service_name
   ```

2. Configure the service to start automatically at startup

   ```
   # systemctl enable name.service
   ```

3. Start the service

   ```
   # systemctl start name.service
   ```

Example

```
# dnf install httpd
# systemctl enable httpd.service
# systemctl start httpd.service
```

## Chapter 20

Firewall

According to dictionary, a firewall is a wall or partition designed to inhibit or prevent the spread of fire. In computer world, firewall is network security system used to secure the incoming and outgoing connections. It prevents unauthorized access to the system. It restricts user to access only designated services.

Fedora Linux kernel has built in firewall, which can be used to allow or deny incoming and outgoing network traffic. To configure firewall, we can do through GUI or manually: -

Firewalld is the new interface firewall in Fedora. It replaces the **iptables** interface and connects to the netfilter kernel code. firewalld stores its rules in various XML files in /usr/lib/firewalld/ and /etc/firewalld/. Firewalld allows security configuration without stopping current configuration. In earlier version with **iptables** every change requires flushing of all old rules and reading new rules from iptable configuration file but in firewalld only new differences are applied without disturbing current connections. Firewalld provides a dynamically managed firewall.

Before configuring firewall here is description of terms used in firewall

Zones

In firewalld concept of zone is based on network interface. All network interfaces can be located in the same default zone or divided into different zones according to the levels of trust defined. By defualt FedoraServer or FedoraWorkstation zone is used for configuration. If you have more than one interface than you can create more zones and restrict trafic between zones. Lets take example if we have web server having two interface one connecting to outside world i.e. public zone and second interface in trusted zone that connects to database server. **Note**: Without any configuration, everything is done by default in the default zone.

Manual Configuration

A command-line client **firewall-cmd**, is provided. It can be used to make permanent and runtime changes to firewall rules. You require be root or administrative privileges to run **firewalld-cmd** command

Install firewalld

```
dnf install firewalld
```

Know if it is running

```
systemctl status firewalld
```
or
```
firewall-cmd --state
```

To display default zone

```
# firewall-cmd --get-default-zone
```

List the available zones

```
# firewall-cmd --get-zones
```

Change the default zone

```
# firewall-cmd --set-default-zone= internal
```

Check the zone interface is associated with

```
# firewall-cmd --get-zone-of-interface=ens33
```

Change the interface zone

```
# firewall-cmd --permanent --zone=internal --change-
interface= ens33
```

List of services in the default zone

```
# firewall-cmd --list-services
```

Add a service to permanently to default zone

```
# firewall-cmd --permanent --add-service=http
```

After that, you have to reload the new configuration

```
# firewall-cmd --reload
```

Add service to specific zone

```
# firewall-cmd --permanent --zone=internal --add-service=http
```

Port Management

Firewalld allows configuration to permit traffic through the firewall to a certain port.

List of ports in the default zone

```
# firewall-cmd --list-ports
```

Opening Port in the Firewall

```
firewall-cmd --permanent --zone=public --add-port=5903/tcp
```

then

```
# firewall-cmd --reload
```

Configuring Services

You can configure the firewall based on a predefined or custom service,

List the services in permanent mode

```
~]# firewall-cmd --get-service --permanent
```

To enable or disable the HTTP service in public zone in permanent mode

```
sudo firewall-cmd --zone=public --add-service=http --
permanent
```

Configuring firewall using GUI

To Configure firewall in GUI, use the GNOME firewall application. If application is not installed by default, you can install it. Press the Windows Button and type firewall. Click on the firewall application.

Configuring Services

start the firewall-config tool and then select Permanent Configuration mode from the drop-down selection menu ,select the network zone whose services are to be configured. Select the Services tab and select the required services by clicking on check box for each service you want to open. Click again to clear the check box to block a service.

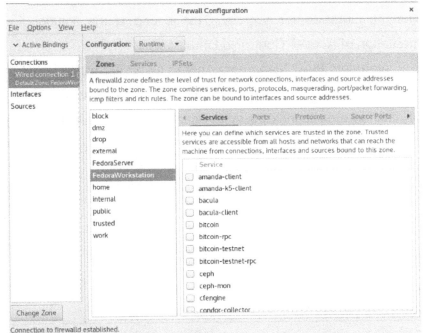

Same way you can zones and interfaces

113

## Chapter 21

Selinux

Selinux is **S**ecurity **E**nhanced **Linux**. Selinux is kernel module that improves the Linux server security. This is one of the solution for implementation of Access Control in Linux.

Selinux implements **MAC** Mandatory Access Control. Selinux is set of security rules, which determine which process can access which file, directory or port etc. Selinux policy to access process, directory, and files is called as context. One goal of Selinux is to protect data and system. Selinux has three forms of access control:

1. Enforcing
2. Permissive
3. Disabled

Enforcing
Selinux denies access based on Selinux policy rules.

Permissive
Selinux does not deny access but denials are logged for the action that would have been denied if running in enforcing mode.

Disabled
Selinux is completely disabled

Check the installation

```
# rpm -qa | grep selinux
```

Check current mode

```
# getenforce
```

Check the status

```
# sestatus
```

Main configuration file

```
/etc/selinux/config
```

To Change the mode

Edit `/etc/Selinux/config` configuration file and change **selinux=enforcing** to desired mode like **selinux= permissive**. After saving the file and reboot the server.

If you set the mode to **permissive** you can check the log what Selinux is doing.

```
# journalctl -xe |grep -i selinux
```

Or

```
tail -f /var/log/audit/audit.log
```

Commands to display context

Description	Command
List process conext	ps auxZ
Display user context	id –Z
Display files with context	ls -lZ
copy wit context	cp -Z
mkdir with context	mkdir -Z

Install selinux

```
# dnf install policycoreutils policycoreutils-python policycoreutils-python-utils
```

Tool to change context

```
# semanage
```

If semanage command is not available run **dnf install policycoreutils policycoreutils-python policycoreutils-python-utils command to** install semanage.

Show context

```
# semanage fcontext -l
```

Types

The main permission control method used in SELinux targeted policy to provide advanced process isolation is **Type Enforcement**. All files and processes are labeled as a type. Types define a SELinux domain for processes and a SELinux type for files

Example of Types are

httpd_sys_content_t

tmp_t

Add context

```
# semanage fcontext -a -t httpd_sys_content_t  /abc/zzz.txt
# ls -Z
-rw-r--r--. root root unconfined_u:object_r:samba_share_t:s0 zzz.txt
```

Set the context to default

```
# restorecon -v -f /abc/zzz.txt
```

Booleans

Booleans allow a part of Selinux policy to change at runtime without any knowledge of Selinux policy writing

List Booleans

```
# semanage boolean -l
```

Configure Booleans

1. list all

```
semanage boolean -l
```

2. list Booleans weather they are on/off

```
getsebool -a
```

3. Allow ftp read and write files in the users home directory

```
setsebool -P ftp_home_dir on
```

4. Check

```
# getsebool ftp_home_dir
ftp_home_dir --> on
```

## Chapter 22

SSH

SSH provides a secure channel over unsecure network in client server architecture. SSH is a replacement of telnet, which is insecure protocol. It allows secure channel to login and execute command securely because all communication between client and server is encrypted.

ssh –x user@hostname

whenever ssh connection is made to system first time the public key of remote system is stored locally so it is identity can be verified next time.

Ctrl + d or exit command will terminate **ssh** session.

If you are connecting form MS windows client to Linux server you require third party software like **putty**.

ssh key

ssh keys helps in identifying yourself to an server using public key cryptography and challenge response authentication. ssh keys are generated in pair one public and private key. The public is for sharing and private key is for you. It must be kept safely.

Server having public key can send challenge, which can only be answered by server holding private key. This allows password less login.

Password less login to server from one server to other server

In this example we will login without password from fedora1 host to host fedora2.

1. Create keys on **fedora1** host

```
[root@fedora1 ~]# ssh-keygen
```

2. Copy public key from **fedora1** to second server **fedora2** host

```
# scp ~/.ssh/id_rsa.pub root@fedora2:/root/id_rsa.server1.pub
```

3. On second server **fedora2** create directory .ssh in the home directory in our case the user is root its home directory is /root and change permissions.

```
[root@fedora2 ~]# mkdir .ssh
[root@fedora2 ~]# chmod 700 .ssh
```

4. Append the public key file to **authorized_keys** file and change permissions.

```
[root@fedora2 ~]# cat id_rsa.server1.pub >> .ssh/authorized_keys
[root@fedora2 ~]# chmod 644 .ssh/authorized_keys
```

5. Now try login form server one i.e **fedora1** to second server i.e. **fedora2** it will not ask for password.

```
[root@fedora1 ~]# ssh root@fedora2
```

## Chapter 23

VNC

VNC Virtual Network Computing is graphical desktop sharing system. Used to get GUI desktop of Linux server remotely. In this VNC client is installed on local machine, which is used to connect to VNC server installed on remote server.

To configure VNC on server whose desktop you want to share

1. install

```
# dnf install tigervnc-server
```

2. Copy file from **/lib/systemd/system/vncserver@.service** to **/etc/systemd/system/vncserver@.service**

```
cp /lib/systemd/system/vncserver@.service
/etc/systemd/system/vncserver@.service
```

3. Edit **/etc/systemd/system/vncserver@.service** change <USER> with the local user which will connect to VNC server

```
[Unit]
Description=Remote desktop service (VNC)
After=syslog.target network.target

[Service]
Type=forking
User=user1

# Clean any existing files in /tmp/.X11-unix environment
```

```
ExecStartPre=-/usr/bin/vncserver -kill %i
ExecStart=/usr/bin/vncserver %i
PIDFile=/home/user1/.vnc/%H%i.pid
ExecStop=-/usr/bin/vncserver -kill %i
```

Change to following in my case it user1

4. Set VNC password

```
# su user_name
$ vncpasswd
```

5. Start VNC server

```
# vncserver :1 -geometry 800x600 -depth 24
```

It will create required files in home directory of user

6. Now stop vnc server

```
vncserver -kill :1
```

7. Open firewall for vncserver

```
firewall-cmd --permanent --add-service vnc-server
firewall-cmd --reload
```

8. Edit file **~/.vnc/xstartup** in home directory of user in my case it is user1 so path is /home/user1/.vnc/xstartup and change **exec /etc/X11/xinit/xinitrc** with **exec /usr/bin/gnome-session** if you are using gnome desktop on the server

```
[root@fedora1 .vnc]# cat xstartup
#!/bin/sh

unset SESSION_MANAGER
unset DBUS_SESSION_BUS_ADDRESS
```

```
#exec /etc/X11/xinit/xinitrc
exec /usr/bin/gnome-session
```

9. Start with display number '1', screen resolution '800x600', color depth '32'

```
[root@fedora1]# vncserver :1 -geometry 800x600 -depth 32
```

10. Install vnc viewer on windows machine I used **realvnc** you can download any free vnc viewer

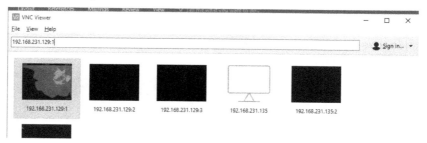

11. Give ipaddress:display number like 192.168.231.128:1 in address box and press enter.

12. It will ask for password we set for vncuser, give password now you can see remote GUI

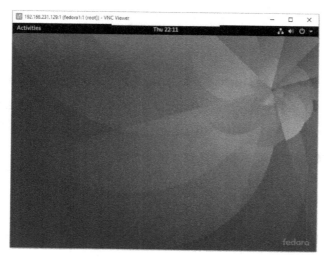

## Chapter 24

FTP

FTP is file transfer protocol. It used to transfer files between the computers on the network. It's based on client server model. There can be three type of client

1. GUI
2. Web browser
3. Command line

In Fedora and derivatives distributions **vsftp** (very secure FTP) Daemon is used as FTP server.

Deploying vsftp

Install the package

```
# dnf install vsftpd
```

Start the server

```
# systemctl start vsftpd
```

Enable the service to start at startup

```
# systemctl enable vsftpd
```

Open the firewall

```
# firewall-cmd --permanent --add-service=ftp
# firewall-cmd --reload
```

Test from remote machine

Syntax

```
# sftp < server IP address or hostname >
```

It will ask for username and password use linux username and password for server

To upload file on ftp prompt

```
sftp> put file_name
```

To download file

```
sftp> get file_name
```

To exit

```
sftp> bye
```

Example

```
[root@fedora2 ~]# sftp fedora1
Connecting to fedora1...
root@fedora1's password:
sftp> pwd
Remote working directory: /root
sftp> cd /etc/
sftp> pwd
Remote working directory: /etc
sftp> get hosts
Fetching /etc/hosts to hosts
/etc/hosts
100%    84      0.1KB/s    00:00
sftp> bye
```

Note You can connect to ftp server anonymously. You can download and upload files to /var/ftp directory.

To configure server to allow anonymous user users edit **/etc/vsftpd/vsftpd.conf**

## Chapter 25

Web server

A webserver is program, which allows web browser clients to access web pages. it uses HTTP (Hypertext Transfer Protocol). In Fedora and its derivatives, Apache HTTP server is used.

Deploying http server

Install http server

```
# dnf install httpd
```

Start service

```
# systemctl start httpd
```

Enable the service to start on boot

```
# systemctl enable httpd
```

Open firewall and reload the configuration

```
# firewall-cmd --permanent --add-service=http
# firewall-cmd --reload
```

Default directory where http keeps contents

/var/www/html

Configuration file

/etc/httpd/conf/http.conf

Test

1. Create file in directory /var/www/html/index.html and Write **Hello**
2. Save the file and exit
3. Open the firefox on the address bar write http://localhost
4. You should see hello

## Chapter 26

Configuring NTP server

It is very important to keep the time of the server to be accurate. When your servers are in production environment it is ideal to keep all servers time in sync. Whenever there is problem in any of the server to correlate the problem with other server the time stamp in the log file is very important.

Fedora you have a choice to use either **ntpd** or **chronyd**. chronyd is ideal for environment where external time references are available intermittently. **chronyd** can perform well even when the network is congested for longer periods of time.

Configuration file
/etc/chrony.conf

In chrony.conf file following are the options
allow

specify a host, subnet, or network from which to allow NTP connections to a machine acting as NTP server. The default is not to allow connections

Server

Give the external time server to sync with

Steps to configure chrony ntp server

1. Install chrony software

```
2. # dnf install -y chrony
```

3. Edit **/etc/chrony.conf** to add the external server to sync with and subnet or client IP address to use to sync with this server

```
#pool 2.fedora.pool.ntp.org iburst
server time.google.com
# Allow NTP client access from local network.
allow 192.168/16
```

4. Start the chrony daemon

```
# systemctl start chronyd
```

5. Enable to start automatically at boot time

```
# systemctl enable chronyd
```

6. Configure firewall to allow NTP service

```
# firewall-cmd --add-service=ntp --permanent
```

After that reload configuration of firewall

```
# firewall-cmd --reload
```

Testing

Check if it is working

```
# chronyc sources
```

```
210 Number of sources = 1
MS Name/IP address          Stratum Poll Reach LastRx Last sample
===============================================================================
^* 216.239.35.12              2   6   377   43   +98us[-1129us] +/-   87ms
```

Or

```
# chronyc  tracking
```

## Chapter 27

Partition and file system

Partitions

Partition is to divide the storage, mostly hard disk into segments in which you can have more than one type of file systems. Partitioning of storage helps in managing storage properly.

fdisk is used to partition the disk.

List the partition table

```
fdisk -l
```

List the partition table for specific

Syntax

```
fdisk -l <device name >
```

Example

```
fdisk -l /dev/hda1
```

Create new partition on device

In this example /dev/sda2 is added to system

1. First check the new device added

```
# fdisk -l
Disk /dev/sdb: 21.5 GB, 21474836480 bytes
255 heads, 63 sectors/track, 2610 cylinders
Units = cylinders of 16065 * 512 = 8225280 bytes
Sector size (logical/physical): 512 bytes / 512 bytes
```

it will show the all storage device

2. Run fdisk on required device using command **fdisk </dev/device_name>**

```
fdisk  /dev/sdb
```

3. Check if partition is there on device selected with disk

   Press **p** and **enter** key

```
Command (m for help): p

Disk /dev/sdb: 21.5 GB, 21474836480 bytes
255 heads, 63 sectors/track, 2610 cylinders, total 41943040
sectors
Units = sectors of 1 * 512 = 512 bytes
Sector size (logical/physical): 512 bytes / 512 bytes
I/O size (minimum/optimal): 512 bytes / 512 bytes
Disk identifier: 0xdec2ee90

   Device Boot      Start         End      Blocks   Id  System
```

4. Press **n** for new partition

5. Press **p** for primary

6. Give partition number like **1, 2, 3, 4**

7. Press **Enter** for starting section

   For last sector, give size like +1G to create 1 GB partition

```
Command (m for help): n
Command action
   e   extended
   p   primary partition (1-4)
p
Partition number (1-4): 1
First sector (2048-41943039, default 2048):
Using default value 2048
Last sector, +sectors or +size{K,M,G} (2048-41943039, default
41943039): +1G
```

8. Press **w** to write on disk

9. List the partition you have created **fisk –l </dev/device_name>**

```
# fdisk -l /dev/sdb


Device      Boot Start      End Sectors Size Id Type
/dev/sdb1        2048 2099199 2097152    1G 83 Linux
```

File system

File System is method used by operating system to store data and retrieve it. File system helps in managing and arranging data. File systems can be

- shareable
- non shareable

XFS

XFS is a high-performance journaling file system that was initially created by Silicon Graphics, Inc. for the IRIX operating system and later ported to Linux. XFS supports metadata journaling, which facilitates quicker crash recovery. The XFS file system can also be defragmented and enlarged while mounted and active. XFS records file system updates asynchronously to a circular buffer (the journal) before it can commit the actual data updates to disk.

EXT File System

Extended file system (ext) is popular file system used in earlier versions of fedora. **Ext3** is journalized file system, it keeps track of changes not yet committed to the file system by recording such changes in data structure to journal which in turn generate circular log. In case of abrupt system down like power failure or crashed file system can be brought back online easily. There are different generation of **ext** File system

- ext2
- ext3
- ext4

.

ext2, ext3   limitation of file system size as 8TB /16TB and file size as 2 TB

Ext4   file size is 16TB. It is efficient reliable and robust.

Creating XFS file system

1. Create partition with fdisk
2. **fdisk -l** check the device name
3. **mkfs -t xfs /dev/sdb1** where **sdb1** is device name and **xfs** is file system type

```
[root@fedora1 ~]# mkfs -t xfs /dev/sdb1
```

4. create mount point

```
[root@fedora1 ~]# mkdir /test1
```

5. Add entry in the /etc/fstab

```
/dev/mapper/fedora-root /     xfs       defaults       0 0
UUID=ad77a812-cece-481e-a935-86ba873384c9 /boot ext4 defaults
1 2
/dev/mapper/fedora-swap swap     swap     defaults       0 0
/dev/sdb2              swap     swap     defaults       0 0
/dev/sdb1   /test1     xfs     defaults       0 2
```

Where **/dev/sdb1** is device **/test1** mount point, **xfs** for partition type, 0 for dump and 2 order for fsck.

134

Removing File System

If you want change the file system or your file system is corrupt and you want new file system on same device first you have to delete the file existing file system. To delete a file system

First unmount the filesystem if it is mounted

Syntax

```
umount <filesystem name>
```

Example

```
# umount /test1
```

Syntax

```
dd if=/dev/zero of=/dev/<device_name> bs=1M count=500000
```

Example

```
dd if=/dev/zero of=/dev/sdb1 bs=1M count=500000
```

Now you can create new file system

Please Note this is destructive process if you have data in the file system please take backup of it before doing this procedure

## Chapter 28

Swap space

Swap space is used in Linux and UNIX to free physical memory. The inactive pages of data is written to slower storage i.e. hard disk. The area where inactive data is written is called as swap space.

Add swap space

1. Create partition

```
[root@fedora1 ~]# fdisk /dev/sdb

WARNING: DOS-compatible mode is deprecated. It's strongly
recommended to switch off the mode (command 'c') and change
display units to sectors (command 'u').

Command (m for help): n
Command action
   e   extended
   p   primary partition (1-4)
p
Partition number (1-4): 2
First cylinder (307-6132, default 307):
Using default value 307
Last cylinder, +cylinders or +size{K,M,G} (307-6132, default
6132): +1G
```

2. Change the type by pressing **t** of partition selected to **82** which is **linux swap**

```
Command (m for help): t
Partition number (1-4): 2
```

```
Hex code (type L to list codes): 82
Changed system type of partition 2 to 82 (Linux swap / Solaris)
```

3. Check the partition

```
Command (m for help): p

Disk /dev/sdb: 21.5 GB, 21474836480 bytes
171 heads, 40 sectors/track, 6132 cylinders
Units = cylinders of 6840 * 512 = 3502080 bytes
Sector size (logical/physical): 512 bytes / 512 bytes
I/O size (minimum/optimal): 512 bytes / 512 bytes
Disk identifier: 0xdec2ee90

   Device Boot      Start         End      Blocks   Id  System
/dev/sdb1               1         307     1048576   83  Linux
/dev/sdb2             307         614     1050280   82  Linux swap / Solaris
```

4. Press w to write partition to disk

```
Command (m for help): w
The partition table has been altered!

Calling ioctl() to re-read partition table.
Syncing disks.
```

5. **mkswap /dev/sdb2** where sdb2 is name of the partition which will be used as swap.

```
[root@fedora1 ~]# mkswap /dev/sdb2
Setting up swapspace version 1, size = 1050276 KiB
no label, UUID=c1f98067-9548-4bf1-843d-5f09f5d5ba56
```

6. Add entry in /etc/fstab

```
/dev/mapper/fedora-root /          xfs      defaults        0 0
UUID=ad77a812a935-86ba873384c9 /boot   ext4 defaults        1 2
/dev/mapper/fedora-swap swap        swap     defaults        0 0
```

```
/dev/sdb2                swap      swap     defaults        0  0
```

7. swapon -a will activate swap

8. swapon -s will show status of all swap space

```
[root@fedora1 ~]# swapon -s
Filename                Type          Size     Used     Priority
/dev/dm-1               partition     2097144 0         -1
/dev/sdb2              partition      1050272 0         -2
```

To deactivate the swap space

```
# swapoff /dev/sdb2
```

## Chapter 29

Logical Volume Manager

In earlier section we learned about creating Linux partition but we can also create partition type LVM (logical partition manager). When we create LVM type partition, LVM manages space allocated to it. Which is more sophisticated than normal Linux partition. LVM has following benefits

- Grow the File system dynamically
- shrink the File system
- Add disk dynamically
- Mirroring
- Stripping
- Snapshot of File system

Terms used in LVM

Physical Volume

Physical Volume (PV) is physical storage unit of an LVM is a block device such as a partition or whole disk. To use the device for an LVM create partition with **fdisk** as **LVM** type.

Volume Groups

One or more physical volumes combined into Volume Group (VG).

Physical Extent

Storage space from Physical Volume is divided in to small unit of fixed size known as physical extent, which is smallest unit that can be allocated. P.E. will same for all physical volume in the same VG.

Logical extent

Logical extent is mapping of PE to make up front end for LVM. By default, one PE is mapped to one LE but, you can map more than one PE to one LE in case of mirroring.

Logical Volume

Logical volume is group of Logical Extent. It is here we create File system. Logical volume is not restricted to physical disk sizes. In addition the hardware storage layer is isolated form software.

Steps to create File system with newly disk added to system

1. Create Physical volume (PV)
   Use **fdisk** command and create partition type Linux LVM **8e**

```
[root@fedora1 ~]# fdisk /dev/sdb

WARNING: DOS-compatible mode is deprecated. It's strongly recommended to
         switch off the mode (command 'c') and change display units
to
         sectors (command 'u').

Command (m for help): n
Command action
   e   extended
   p   primary partition (1-4)
p
Partition number (1-4): 3
First cylinder (615-6132, default 615):
Using default value 615
Last cylinder, +cylinders or +size{K,M,G} (615-6132, default 6132):
+5G

Command (m for help): t
Partition number (1-4): 3
```

```
Hex code (type L to list codes): 8e
Changed system type of partition 3 to 8e (Linux LVM)

Command (m for help): p

Disk /dev/sdb: 21.5 GB, 21474836480 bytes
171 heads, 40 sectors/track, 6132 cylinders
Units = cylinders of 6840 * 512 = 3502080 bytes
Sector size (logical/physical): 512 bytes / 512 bytes
I/O size (minimum/optimal): 512 bytes / 512 bytes
Disk identifier: 0xdec2ee90

   Device Boot      Start         End      Blocks   Id  System
/dev/sdb1              1         307     1048576   83  Linux
/dev/sdb2            307         614     1050280   82  Linux swap /
Solaris
/dev/sdb3            615        2148     5246280   8e  Linux LVM

Command (m for help): w
The partition table has been altered!

Calling ioctl() to re-read partition table.

WARNING: Re-reading the partition table failed with error 16: Device
or resource busy.
The kernel still uses the old table. The new table will be used at
the next reboot or after you run partprobe(8) or kpartx(8)
Syncing disks.
```

2. Reboot the server

3. Create PV using command **pvcreate _device_name_** where _device_name_ is device created with fdisk

```
[root@fedora1 ~]# pvcreate /dev/sdb3
   Physical volume "/dev/sdb3" successfully created
[root@fedora1 ~]# pvdisplay /dev/sdb3
  "/dev/sdb3" is a new physical volume of "5.00 GiB"
  --- NEW Physical volume ---
  PV Name               /dev/sdb3
  VG Name
  PV Size               5.00 GiB
```

141

Allocatable	NO
PE Size	0
Total PE	0
Free PE	0
Allocated PE	0
PV UUID	EQ7ElZ-WiGK-Z0m5-5gSN-gP95-MFSk-pKyTvS

4. Create Volume Group (VG)
   vgcreate *VG_name PV_name*

```
[root@fedora1 ~]# vgcreate vg01 /dev/sdb3
  Volume group "vg01" successfully created
```

5. Create new Logical Volume(LV)
   lvcreate -n *LV_name* -L *size VG_name*

```
[root@fedora1 ~]# lvcreate -n lv01 -L 1G vg01
  Logical volume "lv01" created
```

6. Create File System on LV
   mkfs -t xfs /dev/*VG_name*/*LV_name*

```
[root@fedora1 ~]# mkfs -t xfs /dev/vg01/lv01
```

7. Check the UUID of newly created file system

```
#  blkid /dev/vg01/lv01
```

8. Make directory to be used as mount point

```
# mkdir /newfs
```

9. Add entry to **/etc/fstab** mount system automatically at startup

```
UUID=6acaa400-541139e830e  /newfs  xfs defaults      1 2
```

10. Mount the file system

```
mount -a
```

PV Commands

Description	Command
Display PV properties	pvdisplay
Show all LVM block devices	pvscan
Prevent allocation of PE on PV	pvchange -xn /dev/PV_name
Remove PV	pvremove /dev/PV_name

Volume Group Commands

Description	Command
Display VG properties	vgdisplay
Display VG List	vgs
Add PV to VG	vgextend vgname /dev/PV_name **Example** `# vgextend vg01 /dev/sdb5`
Remove PV form VG	vgreduce vg1 /dev/PV_name **Example** `# vgreduce vg01 /dev/sdb5`
Activating VG	vgchange -ay VG_name
deactivating VG	vgchange -ay VG_name
Remove VG	vgremove VG_name **Example** `vgremove /dev/vg02`
Recreate a VG Directory	vgmknodes

Moving Volume group from one system to other

1. On first system where VG is currently running unmount all FS which is part of VG

```
umount /newfs
```

2. Deactivate the VG
   Syntax

```
vgchange -an VG_name
```

   Example

```
[root@fedora1 /]# vgchange -an sharedvg
```

3. Export the VG with **vgexport VG_name** command

```
[root@fedora1 /]# vgexport sharedvg
```

4. After attaching HDD to new system import the VG with **vgimport VG_name** command

```
[root@fedora2 ~]# vgimport sharedvg
```

5. Activate the VG with **vgchange -ay VG_name**

```
[root@fedora2 ~]# vgchange -ay sharedvg
```

6. Mount the file systems on the VG

```
[root@fedora2 ~]# mount /dev/sharedvg/sharedlv /mnt
```

7. Check the contents of file system

```
[root@fedora2 ~]# cd /mnt
```

Extending FileSystem

1. Check the current FS size
   df -h /fsname

```
/dev/mapper/vg01-lv01        1008M   34M  924M   4% /newfs
```

2. Check if you have enough free space i.e free PE on the VG where LV of FS you want extend is there.

```
[root@fedora1 ~]# vgdisplay vg01
   --- Volume group ---
   VG Name               vg01
   System ID
   Format                lvm2
   Metadata Areas        1
   Metadata Sequence No  5
   VG Access             read/write
   VG Status             resizable
   MAX LV                0
   Cur LV                1
   Open LV               1
   Max PV                0
   Cur PV                1
   Act PV                1
```

145

```
VG Size              5.00 GiB
PE Size              4.00 MiB
Total PE             1280
Alloc PE / Size      256 / 1.00 GiB
Free  PE / Size      1024 / 4.00 GiB
VG UUID              EXKfhW-MfE4-4ZtU-uQuM-v9e4-AJ9k-
Uo6z4B
```

3. Extend   the   Logical   Volume   **lvextend   -L   size**
   /dev/vgname/lvname

```
[root@fedora1 ~]# lvextend -L +200M /dev/vg01/lv01
  Extending logical volume lv01 to 1.20 GiB
  Logical volume lv01 successfully resized
```

4. Extend the file system using

xfs_growfs /fsname

```
[root@fedora1 ~]# xfs_growfs /newfs
```

5. Check the FS size
   df -h /fsname

```
/dev/mapper/vg01-lv01     1.2G   34M   1.1G   3% /newfs
```

Reduce the File System

1. Check the current FS size
   df -h /fs_name

```
/dev/mapper/vg01-lv01     1.2G   34M   1.1G   3% /newfs
```

146

2. Backup the File System

```
# xfsdump -f /tmp/newfs.dump /newfs
```

3. unmount the Filesystem
   umount /fs_name

```
# umount /newfs
```

4. Remove the LV

```
# lvremove /dev/mapper/vg01-lv01
```

5. Recreate LV

```
#lvcreate -n lv01 -L 1G vg01
```

6. Recreate the File system

```
# mkfs.xfs /dev/vg01/lv01
```

7. First check the UUID

```
# blkid /dev/vg01/lv01
```

8. Change the UUID of File system in /etc/fstab

9. Mount File System

```
# mount -a
```

10. Restore the backup

```
xfsrestore -f /tmp/newfs.dump /newfs
```

11. Check File System

```
#   df -h /newfs
```

## Chapter 30

LVM snapshot

LVM snapshot is a point in time copy of Logical Volume. The snapshot provides static view of original volume. Once snapshot has been taken we can use this snapshot to take backup volume as snapshot is static copy and it will not change while backup is happening unlike the original volume which is dynamic.

The snapshot volume size should be enough to store the data that will change after snapshot has been taken. the volume will store only changes after the snapshot has been taken.

Create snapshot LV

1. Check the LV name and size of File System for which you want to create snapshot

```
[root@fedora1 /]# df -h /newfs
Filesystem            Size  Used Avail Use% Mounted on
/dev/mapper/vg01-lv01   1008M   34M  924M   4% /newfs
```

2. Check you have space at least equivalent to 10% of file system you want to take snapshot available on the VG where original LV is located

```
# vgdisplay vg01
```

3. Create LV 8 to 10 % of capicity of original LV
   lvcreate -s -n snaplvname -L size /dev/vgname/orginal_lv_name

```
# lvcreate -s -n snaplv1 -L 100M /dev/mapper/vg01-lv01
```

4. Create mount point

```
# mkdir /snapfs
```

5. if you want to see content of snapshot LV
   mount -o ro /dev/vgname/snaplv /mount_point_snaplv

```
# mount -o ro /dev/vg01/snaplv1 /snapfs/
```

If you have xfs file system then the UUID of snapshot LV and original

LV is same you have give following command to mount

```
mount -t xfs -o ro -onouuid /dev/vg01/snaplv1 /snapfs/
```

6. Change to directory to check the contents
   cd /mount_point_snaplv

```
# cd /snapfs/
# ls
```

Remove snapshot LV

1. Unmount snap File system
   umount /mount_point_snaplv

```
[root@fedora1 /]# umount /snapfs
```

2. Remove the snap logical
   lvremove /dev/vgname/snaplv

```
[root@fedora1 /]# lvremove /dev/mapper/vg01-snaplv1
```

## Chapter 31

Boot process

Boot process of Linux

1. **BIOS**

2. **Master Boot Record**

3. **GRUB 2**

    Uses /boot/grub2/grub.cfg to select the kernel image. Do not edit this file. GRUB2 menu-configuration settings uses /etc/default/grub when generating grub.cfg

4. **Kernel**

    a. Mounts the root file system as specified in the "root=" in grub.conf

    b. The kernel starts the systemd process with a process ID of 1 (PID 1)

    c. **initrd** stands for Initial RAM Disk. initrd is used by kernel as temporary root file system until kernel is booted and the real root file system is mounted. It also contains drivers, which are required to access hard disk and other necessary hardware.

5. **systemd**

Systemd is a system and service manager for Linux operating systems. It is designed to be backwards compatible with SysV init scripts, and provides a number of features such as parallel startup of system services at boot time .systemd is the parent process of all processes on a system.

systemd reads **/etc/systemd/system/default.target** to determine the default system target earlier it used to called as run level. After determining the target, it performs the initialization of system, which includes

1. Setting the host name
2. Initializing the network
3. Initializing the system hardware
4. Mounting the file systems
5. Starting swapping

## Chapter 32

Reset unknown root password

1. At menu press any key any key to enter GRUB menu press arrow keys to stop count down

2. Select first item not the recovery and press **e**

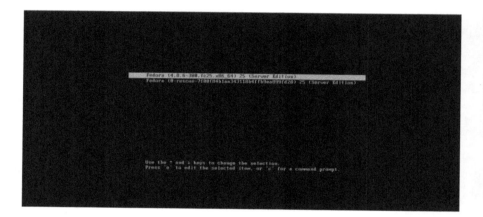

3. Look for line initrd16 above it at the last of line write **rd.break** press Ctrl + x key

4. It will give prompt but root file system is read only

```
switch_root:/# mount
rootfs on / type rootfs (rw)
proc on /proc type proc (rw,nosuid,nodev,noexec,relatime)
sysfs on /sys type sysfs (rw,nosuid,nodev,noexec,relatime)
devtmpfs on /dev type devtmpfs (rw,nosuid,size=926092k,nr_inodes=231523,mode=755)
securityfs on /sys/kernel/security type securityfs (rw,nosuid,nodev,noexec,relatime)
tmpfs on /dev/shm type tmpfs (rw,nosuid,nodev)
devpts on /dev/pts type devpts (rw,nosuid,noexec,relatime,gid=5,mode=620,ptmxmode=000)
tmpfs on /run type tmpfs (rw,nosuid,nodev,mode=755)
tmpfs on /sys/fs/cgroup type tmpfs (rw,nosuid,nodev,noexec,mode=755)
cgroup on /sys/fs/cgroup/systemd type cgroup (rw,nosuid,nodev,noexec,relatime,xattr,release_ag
pstore on /sys/fs/pstore type pstore (rw,nosuid,nodev,noexec,relatime)
cgroup on /sys/fs/cgroup/cpuset type cgroup (rw,nosuid,nodev,noexec,relatime,cpuset)
cgroup on /sys/fs/cgroup/cpu,cpuacct type cgroup (rw,nosuid,nodev,noexec,relatime,cpuacct,cpu
cgroup on /sys/fs/cgroup/memory type cgroup (rw,nosuid,nodev,noexec,relatime,memory)
cgroup on /sys/fs/cgroup/devices type cgroup (rw,nosuid,nodev,noexec,relatime,devices)
cgroup on /sys/fs/cgroup/freezer type cgroup (rw,nosuid,nodev,noexec,relatime,freezer)
cgroup on /sys/fs/cgroup/net_cls type cgroup (rw,nosuid,nodev,noexec,relatime,net_cls)
cgroup on /sys/fs/cgroup/blkio type cgroup (rw,nosuid,nodev,noexec,relatime,blkio)
cgroup on /sys/fs/cgroup/perf_event type cgroup (rw,nosuid,nodev,noexec,relatime,perf_event)
cgroup on /sys/fs/cgroup/hugetlb type cgroup (rw,nosuid,nodev,noexec,relatime,hugetlb)
configfs on /sys/kernel/config type configfs (rw,relatime)
/dev/mapper/rhel_rhl-one-root on /sysroot type xfs (ro,relatime,attr2,inode64,noquota)
switch_root:/#
```

5. Mount the / root file system in read write mode

```
switch_root:/# mount -o remount,rw /sysroot
```

6. Chroot /sysroot

```
switch_root:/# chroot /sysroot
```

7. Give **passwd** command to change password

8. If you Selinux is installed create file

```
sh-4.2# touch /.autorelabel
```

9. Write **exit** and press enter

10. Write **exit** and press enter again to start the system in normal mode

## Chapter 33

Identify your system

Know version of Fedora

```
# cat /etc/fedora-release
```

Know running kernel version

```
# uname -r
```
or
```
# cat /proc/version
```

List all installed kernel version

```
# dnf list installed kernel\*
```

Display CPU information

```
# lscpu
```
or
```
# cat /proc/cpuinfo
```

Detailed description of system hardware

```
# dmidecode
```

Display memory information

```
# cat /proc/meminfo
```
or
```
# free -m          shows memory in MB
```

lists all PCI devices present in the system

```
[root@fedora1 ~]# lspci
00:00.0 Host bridge: Intel Corporation 440BX/ZX/DX - 82443BX/ZX/DX Host bridge
(rev 01)
00:01.0 PCI bridge: Intel Corporation 440BX/ZX/DX - 82443BX/ZX/DX AGP bridge (rev
01)
00:07.0 ISA bridge: Intel Corporation 82371AB/EB/MB PIIX4 ISA (rev 08)
00:07.1 IDE interface: Intel Corporation 82371AB/EB/MB PIIX4 IDE (rev 01)
00:07.3 Bridge: Intel Corporation 82371AB/EB/MB PIIX4 ACPI (rev 08)
00:07.7 System peripheral: VMware Virtual Machine Communication Interface (rev
10)
00:0f.0 VGA compatible controller: VMware SVGA II Adapter
00:10.0 SCSI storage controller: LSI Logic / Symbios Logic 53c1030 PCI-X Fusion-
MPT Dual Ultra320 SCSI (rev 01)
00:11.0 PCI bridge: VMware PCI bridge (rev 02)
(Output is truncated)
```

List all usb devices

```
# lsusb
```

List block device

```
# lsblk
```

List all partitions

```
# fdisk -l
```

List CPU, Memory, Process

```
# top
```

Display Hostname

```
# hostname
```

sosreport

The "**sosreport**" is a tool to collect troubleshooting data on fedora systems. It generates report of configuration of Linux system and most important logs in tarball compressed format which can be used for any problem or performance issues.

Install package

```
# dnf install sos
# dnf install abrt-cli
```

Generate report

```
# sosreport
```

It prompts for the name of file and logged case number for which you are generating report. If you do not have case number.

## Chapter 34

System Monitoring Tools

Viewing system processes

ps

Display report of running process. It is a snapshot of the current processes at time of running command.

To see every process on the system and thire owner

```
ps aux
```

To list all related threads after each process

```
ps axms
```

Top

top command displays processor activity of Linux machine The top command displays list of running processes on the system It also displays additional information about current usage of CPU, memory and swap space.

```
# top

top - 21:59:05 up  5:58,  3 users,  load average: 0.16, 0.03, 0.01
Tasks: 188 total,  1 running, 187 sleeping,  0 stopped,  0 zombie
%Cpu(s):  0.0 us,  0.7 sy,  0.0 ni, 97.7 id,  1.0 wa,  0.3 hi,  0.3 si,  0.0 st
KiB Mem :  2045748 total,   168512 free,  1038120 used,   839116 buff/cache
KiB Swap:  2097148 total,  1906704 free,   190444 used.   891936 avail Mem


  PID USER      PR  NI    VIRT    RES    SHR S %CPU %MEM     TIME+ COMMAND
 1771 root      20   0  406112  10888   7084 S  0.3  0.5   0:30.40 vmtoolsd
 5854 root      20   0  156652   3960   3456 R  0.3  0.2   0:00.03 top
    1 root      20   0  215220   8316   5820 S  0.0  0.4   0:09.58 systemd
```

157

2	root	20	0	0	0	0	S	0.0	0.0	0:00.03 kthreadd
3	root	20	0	0	0	0	S	0.0	0.0	0:02.07 ksoftirqd/0
5	root	0	-20	0	0	0	S	0.0	0.0	0:00.00 kworker/0:0H
7	root	20	0	0	0	0	S	0.0	0.0	0:01.05 rcu_sched
8	root	20	0	0	0	0	S	0.0	0.0	0:00.00 rcu_bh
9	root	20	0	0	0	0	S	0.0	0.0	0:01.07 rcuos/0
10	root	20	0	0	0	0	S	0.0	0.0	0:00.00 rcuob/0
11	root	rt	0	0	0	0	S	0.0	0.0	0:00.00 migration/0
12	root	0	-20	0	0	0	S	0.0	0.0	0:00.00 lru-add-drain
13	root	rt	0	0	0	0	S	0.0	0.0	0:00.09 watchdog/0
14	root	20	0	0	0	0	S	0.0	0.0	0:00.00 cpuhp/0
15	root	20	0	0	0	0	S	0.0	0.0	0:00.00 kdevtmpfs
16	root	0	-20	0	0	0	S	0.0	0.0	0:00.00 netns
17	root	20	0	0	0	0	S	0.0	0.0	0:00.00 oom_reaper
18	root	0	-20	0	0	0	S	0.0	0.0	0:00.00 writeback
19	root	20	0	0	0	0	S	0.0	0.0	0:00.11 kcompactd0
20	root	25	5	0	0	0	S	0.0	0.0	0:00.00 ksmd

System Monitor Tool

System monitor tool is GUI tool for system monitoring. The Processes tab allows you to view, search for, change the priority of, and kill processes. In search bar on desktop type system monitor. Click Processes tab to view the list of running processes.

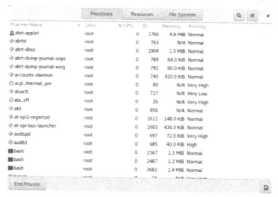

Click resources tab to check CPU, memory and Swap space utilization.

It also shows network activities.

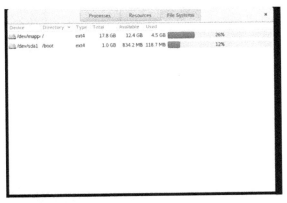

File system tab give information about file system type, total size, available, used and percentage used.

Free

Free command provides information about system memory and swap space

```
[root@fedora1 ~]# free
              total        used        free      shared  buff/cache   available
Mem:        2045748     1066888      135120        7596      843740      863048
Swap:       2097148      193704     1903444
```

To view memory in Megabytes

```
# free -m
```

lsblk

The **blkid** command displays information about available block devices which includes block device's major and minor number, size, type and mount point.

```
[root@fedora1 ~]# lsblk -a
NAME              MAJ:MIN RM  SIZE RO TYPE MOUNTPOINT
sr0                11:0    1 1024M  0 rom
sda                 8:0    0   20G  0 disk
├─sda2              8:2    0   19G  0 part
│ ├─fedora-swap 253:1    0    2G  0 lvm  [SWAP]
│ └─fedora-root 253:0    0   17G  0 lvm  /
└─sda1              8:1    0    1G  0 part /boot
```

To get UUID of a block device

```
[root@fedora1 ~]# blkid /dev/sda1
/dev/sda1: UUID="b4bd566c-8591-4695-a55f-28335f914a11" TYPE="ext4"
PARTUUID="f2acf7d4-01"
```

Partx

The **partx** command display a list of disk partitions.

To display list of partition for a device

```
[root@fedora1 ~]# partx -s /dev/sda
NR    START      END  SECTORS SIZE NAME UUID
 1     2048  2099199  2097152   1G       f2acf7d4-01
 2  2099200 41943039 39843840  19G       f2acf7d4-02
```

160

findmnt

The **findmnt** command allows you to list all mounted file systems

```
[root@fedora1 ~]# findmnt
TARGET                              SOURCE      FSTYPE      OPTIONS
/                                   /dev/mapper/fedora-root
| ext4              rw,relatime,seclabel,data-ordered
├─/sys                              sysfs       sysfs       rw,nosuid,nodev,noexec,relatime,seclabel
| ├─/sys/kernel/security            securityfs  securityfs  rw,nosuid,nodev,noexec,relatime
|  ├─/sys/fs/cgroup                                         tmpfs       tmpfs
ro,nosuid,nodev,noexec,seclabel,size=498584k,nr_inodes=124646,mode=755
|   |   ├─/sys/fs/cgroup/systemd                            cgroup      cgroup
rw,nosuid,nodev,noexec,relatime,xattr,release_agent=/usr/lib/systemd/systemd-cgroups-agent,name=systemd
| | ├─/sys/fs/cgroup/perf_event     cgroup      cgroup      rw,nosuid,nodev,noexec,relatime,perf_event
| | ├─/sys/fs/cgroup/hugetlb        cgroup      cgroup      rw,nosuid,nodev,noexec,relatime,hugetlb
| | ├─/sys/fs/cgroup/devices        cgroup      cgroup      rw,nosuid,nodev,noexec,relatime,devices
| | ├─/sys/fs/cgroup/pids           cgroup      cgroup      rw,nosuid,nodev,noexec,relatime,pids
| | ├─/sys/fs/cgroup/freezer        cgroup      cgroup      rw,nosuid,nodev,noexec,relatime,freezer
| | ├─/sys/fs/cgroup/memory         cgroup      cgroup      rw,nosuid,nodev,noexec,relatime,memory
| | ├─/sys/fs/cgroup/cpuset         cgroup      cgroup      rw,nosuid,nodev,noexec,relatime,cpuset
| | ├─/sys/fs/cgroup/blkio          cgroup      cgroup      rw,nosuid,nodev,noexec,relatime,blkio
| | ├─/sys/fs/cgroup/cpu,cpuacct    cgroup      cgroup      rw,nosuid,nodev,noexec,relatime,cpu,cpuacct
| | ├─/sys/fs/cgroup/net_cls,net_prio cgroup    cgroup      rw,nosuid,nodev,noexec,relatime,net_cls,net_prio
| ├─/sys/fs/pstore                  pstore      pstore      rw,nosuid,nodev,noexec,relatime,seclabel
| ├─/sys/fs/selinux                 selinuxfs   selinuxfs   rw,relatime
| ├─/sys/kernel/debug               debugfs     debugfs     rw,relatime,seclabel
| ├─/sys/kernel/config              configfs    configfs    rw,relatime
| └─/sys/fs/fuse/connections        fusectl     fusectl     rw,relatime
├─/proc                             proc        proc        rw,nosuid,nodev,noexec,relatime
|    ├─/proc/sys/fs/binfmt_misc                             systemd-1   autofs
rw,relatime,fd=27,pgrp=1,timeout=0,minproto=5,maxproto=5,direct,pipe_ino=14129
| └─/proc/fs/nfsd                   nfsd        nfsd        rw,relatime
(Out put is truncated)
```

du

The **du** command allows you to display disk usage by files in a directory

```
[root@fedora1 ~]# du
4         ./Templates
4         ./Music
4         ./.pki/nssdb
8         ./.pki
24        ./.gnupg
```

To display output in human readable format i.e. the size in KB and MB

```
[root@fedora1 ~]# du -h
4.0K    ./Templates
4.0K    ./Music
4.0K    ./.pki/nssdb
8.0K    ./.pki
24K     ./.gnupg
4.0K    ./Videos
4.0K    ./Pictures
4.0K    ./Public
4.0K    ./.config/gconf
4.0K    ./.config/gnome-boxes/sources
8.0K    ./.config/gnome-boxes
4.0K    ./.config/abrt
12K     ./.config/dconf
4.0K    ./.config/gnome-session/saved-session
```

Display summary

```
[root@fedora1 ~]# du -sh
9.1M    .
```

df

The **df** command displays report of file system disk space usage.

To display the disk space usage by each file system

```
[root@fedora1 ~]# df -h
Filesystem          Size  Used Avail Use% Mounted on
devtmpfs            476M     0  476M   0% /dev
tmpfs               487M  336K  487M   1% /dev/shm
tmpfs               487M  2.4M  485M   1% /run
tmpfs               487M     0  487M   0% /sys/fs/cgroup
```

www.ingramcontent.com/pod-product-compliance
Lightning Source LLC
Chambersburg PA
CBHW031240050326
40690CB00007B/880